Dealing With It

Six Years of Mourning, Medals and Men

Gemma Spofforth

For Mum

THANKS

Cover Artwork and Photography: Zachary Scheffer & Scott Rosser

Co-author: Craig Lord, ghost-writer, journalist and friend, is the swimming correspondent of The Times and Sunday Times and Editor of SwimVortex.com

"My sincere thanks and love go to the people who helped me on my journey and with this work. Those not named will know who they are." - Gemma

Contents

Introduction

A tiny embryo swimming in the vastness of a mother's uterus, growing vicariously, hidden beneath a protective barrier, a protective cocoon of relentless love and affection from a woman full of life and vitality, fiercely defensive of her tiny swimmer.

In writing this book I, that tiny embryo, want to take you on my journey. I want to take you through my reality and share a rollercoaster of a life. I will share my utmost highs and my deepest lows, the experience as I felt it, the experience as I lived it for the past six years of my life.

The individuality of one's life, the experiences and struggles become intrinsic to growth and being. Frederick Perls once said:

I do my thing and you do your thing
I am not in this world to
live up to your expectations,
and you are not in this world to
live up to mine.
You are you
and I am I
and if by chance we find each other,
it's beautiful.

I write to you and for you, I write to explain my growth, my maturity, my tragedy and my healing. If you can relate to the story, I write to offer solace, empathy or clarity. I write with the knowledge that your journey, your demons, however big or small, are as central to your character, to your personality, as mine were and are to me.

CHAPTER 1

A Doctor's Mistake.

"Sometimes we can choose the paths we follow. Sometimes our choices are made for us. And sometimes we have no choice at all"

— NEIL GAIMAN

The weeks go by so slowly. The prescribed food poisoning continues to take its toll, a little more weight lost each day. Her pale blue eyes weaken, the soul sapped from them. Late at night, the vomiting keeps her awake, the sound of retching muffled as she tries so hard not to disturb anyone else in the house. She leaves her bed so as not to wake her husband of 24 years and lays down in the spare room next to mine. Her gagging wakes me from a peaceful slumber.

When I pluck up the courage to go through to see if she needs anything, she is lying there with the sick bowl perched on her lap. Her short brown hair drips with sweat; her eyes are scorched with sleeplessness, their blueness masked by the grey of a vacant stare. It is as if her very life is being sucked away before my eyes.

Here is the woman who gave birth to me, the pillar of strength who has only ever cried twice in front of me. She is the strength that guides me through life, Mum to my brother Peter. She is Dorothy Lesley Spofforth, love of the life of David Mark Spofforth, our Dad.

Her life, it seems, is hanging by a thread as the rest of the world rolls on, time ticking mercilessly, regardless. I drive to the swimming pool at 4:30 in the morning. By the time a long workout is done, early rays burn the horizon ochre and orange. Sunrise is a second start to the day for a swimmer. I drive to school under a brightening sky. Calculus, music, physics and then I leave school smarter than I arrived, homeward bound, but not before another workout in the pool.

Exhausted from the long day, the drive home is just an automatic routine now, one I could do with my eyes closed as each bend in the road becomes more familiar with every passing training session. Each day reinforces the same habits as the one before. Almost forgetting the previous night's horrors, I return home to my favourite meal: spaghetti bolognaise drowned with tomato ketchup and grated cheddar cheese. Ahead of me is another round of homework, television and instant messaging to the same friends with whom I have just spent the day.

I'm in my routine. Events are about to take a different turn.

Mum has been to see the doctor again. She's been given a new diagnosis for the strange illness that has plagued her of late and caused the weight to fall off her. She has not been able to keep down a meal for almost three weeks. Now, she sits in front of the television, an empty expression on her face, and asks me to settle down beside her. She has something important to tell me.

∗ ∗ ∗

I had always been a swimmer. My primary school, Arundale School in Pulborough, Sussex, printed a magazine in 1997 when I was aged 10. The swimming report recounts a match against another local school, Westbourne House, which was later to be my brother's school and which kindly offered me swimming facilities when I needed them.

The report read: ".The pool was filled with the excited support of both parents and children as both teams fought to the last length. Arundale just came home first, thanks to the brilliant swimming of Gemma Spofforth. Well done Gemma, I am glad you were swimming for Arundale!"

Swimming wasn't my only sport. I loved netball, and my height - above my peers on my way to a touch over 6ft - gave me an advantage when it came to accuracy with the ball.

My career as a serious athlete started when I was 13. I won the 50m and 100m backstroke at the British National Age Group Championships in 2001 when I was coached by Chris Adams at Bognor Regis Swimming Club. The sport took over my life. My parents, teachers and school friends knew that swimming came first as I headed along a path known to many athletes: a gruelling training regime, and a competition history characterised by turbulent waves of elation at winning and crushing disappointment at failure. For many years, I came second more often than not.

Life was lived for the thrill of soaring moments such as that when I took national success into international waters and claimed that same 50m title at the European Junior Championships in 2003 under the guidance of coach Chris Nesbit at the Portsmouth Northsea club. That same year another pupil of his, Katy Sexton, became the first British woman ever to win a senior World title in an Olympic-sized pool (50 metres long) when she won the 200m backstroke at global championships in Barcelona.

The dedication required and the drive I felt were hardly the stuff of what many would call a "normal" childhood. I gave up playing the piano and the clarinet. I stopped playing netball and bypassed skiing in case I injured an ankle. I gave up any sort of traditional social life and ploughed energy, heart and soul into the pool.

Great opportunities followed, with great frequency. I travelled the world and my ambition took me to 21 countries; to Australia and back via four continents, each passing place and culture seen through the goggles of a life less ordinary. I have heard it said that athletes "sacrifice" their childhoods. I see it differently. I would not trade my childhood for another.

Time management was very important from an early age. Mum was the official timekeeper who helped me immensely along the way. A full-time mathematics teacher to 16-to-19 year-olds and full-time mother of two, she was chief organiser for the whole family, multi-tasking with ease, constantly reminding us of a meeting, a schoolbook that might otherwise have been forgotten or the date of an exam. She packed our lunches the night before we needed them, cooking the pasta and leaving it to cool over the sink, chopping bits of salad and covering my dish with salad cream whilst leaving my brother's plain. In all the countless times she repeated the exercise, only once did she mix up the lunches so that my brother got the salad cream he wouldn't eat.

Each evening, no matter how busy she was organising the local netball league, marking papers or preparing lesson plans, she would place both our lunches in the fridge. Each morning she would add them to a packet of crisps, an apple and a yogurt for each of us, wrap them in a plastic bag and pack them in our school bags. My bag was left in her car so I could collect it on my walk from the pool to my school past the school where she taught.

Managing time never seemed complicated: everything was done for me. Mum arranged my life, taught me how to prioritise, and make choices, my coach organised most of my swimming, and if he didn't Mum arranged that too. Even my teachers treated me leniently when it came to schoolwork because I was "a swimmer".

After setting a best time of 1min 02.83sec over 100m backstroke in 2003, at the age of 15, the best I could manage at Olympic Trials the following year was a 1:04.13, the pressure of trials and the tricky transition from junior to senior waters contributing to a poor performance. Training with Katy Sexton I saw and understood what it took to be a champion and to make the grade: daily devotion, excellence a habit each day, each session and exercise part of a bigger picture and a process aimed at bringing everything together for peak performance some years down the line.

In 2004, I was not going to make it: I crumpled back to the junior that I thought I had left behind. There is a reason for all things and the experience of falling shy lit a flame of desire in me: I wanted to do better; I wanted to show that I had something better to give.

I started to understand the extent to which swimming could open many doors and opportunities when I competed in the British Open Championships in 2005. The competition served as selection trials for the World Championships held every two years in pools 50m long and the most important event on the swimming calendar after the Olympic Games.

I would no longer be racing only those in my own age group but rivals of all ages. I won the 50 and 100 metres backstroke titles. I was the fastest female backstroke specialist in the country, bar none. I finished ahead of one of Britain's two Olympic representatives of 2004, Sarah Price. My transition to senior racing had started in earnest, making the world-championship team bound for Montreal in July 2005 allowed me to take one step closer to my ultimate dream: the Olympic Games.

Although my time in the 100m, a best of 1min 02.29, was not fast enough to earn automatic selection to an individual swim at the world champion-ships in Montreal, it was good enough to put me in the medley relay. Once in

Canada, I was allowed to race the individual event and finished 33rd a couple of seconds from best.

It was a start. I had made it to the world stage. The training, the day-after-day routine of monotonous cardiovascular workouts in the pool, fitting everything in with school, was starting to pay off. All of this was only possible with the support and understanding of my parents, their love often taking them beyond the call in their efforts to help me to chase my dreams, to honour my ambition and promise. I was blessed with parents who did not hesitate to help in any circumstance.

At 4:07am after the night on which Mum had asked me to sit down because she had something important to tell me, I drive over a log in the driveway, get it stuck between the suspension and the wheel of my little black Toyota Yaris. There is only one place to turn to. My Dad doesn't hesitate to get out of bed on a pitch-black and snowy morn and drive me the 45 minutes it takes to get to the pool before what would be a long day at the office for him.

Like most teenagers, I am self-focused at this point in my life. My mind is on my own troubles. It is definitely the worst day to make it through without a car. The top two years at school are due to spend a day in the middle of a forest, bonding. I arrange to drive to the woods to meet the group there after morning training and have permission to leave the bonding day a little early to get back to the pool in time for afternoon workout.

Events force a change in plans: I walk to school after swim practice, catch the bus to the New Forest and then take a taxi for an hour back to the pool in the afternoon. By some miracle, I manage to make it through the day, tears rolling down my face until I force myself to embrace the bonding day and set sadness aside. For a while, I forget what my Mum told me last night. Back at the pool, practice goes by a lot slower than usual: I keep asking myself why this is happening to Mum? Why now? Why us?

On the way home from training, silence replaces the radio sing-a-long that I would otherwise have enjoyed with Dad. When he finally speaks, he tells me that my car will take about a week to fix and in the meantime he will take me to and from practice at four in the morning and home again at 6.30 each evening.

His kindness is all it takes. My eyes stream. I can barely see the cars in front of us. I try so hard to hide my tears from him. There is something surreal about the journey home and the superficial questions that follow what is turning into the most intense moment of our lives. My mouth moves, words emerge but nonsense flows between us.

Dealing With It

The heavy raindrops that beat down on the windscreen only add to the miserable weight of it all. My emotions are raw. When we get home, I am still crying as I peer at my damaged car in the driveway. Dad notices the tears and says that there really are much bigger problems in the world to worry about. His misunderstanding angers me. Only later will I learn that he and Mum had entered a pact not to tell us her news until it became too obvious to ignore; here in the driveway, Dad has no idea that I already know what's happening.

I am not thinking about the car. That is not why I am crying. Questions race through my head. How am I supposed to deal with the weight that Mum has just placed on my shoulders? If I feel this broken, how are my 15-year-old brother and my Dad going to cope? How could he think that I'm crying because of the car? Surely he is living through the same pain, even if men don't express their emotions in the same way?

I need to get indoors, I need to give Mum a hug, tell her how much I love her. Only when faced with tragedy do you realise how important the little things mean. A hug can say so much. And that is all I have to give.

We sit and stare at the television, let the cheeriness of a show wash over us, nothing able to break the awkward silence between a mother and her daughter. We are both lost for words, stunned by a situation that none of us knows how to handle.

I hold her close to me, never wanting to let go. A week from now, her first hospital appointment is due. First diagnosed as food poisoning, a sickness that has lasted weeks has revealed a darker truth: bowel cancer. My Mum has cancer.

Chapter 2

Hospital

"You never know how much you really believe anything until its truth or falsehood becomes a matter of life and death to you"

– C.S. LEWIS

The days fly by, life is monotonous. There's swimming, school, friends and family. I count the seconds to the moment Mum will have the operation and lose count of the people who have comforted me, shared their stories as a way of offering support. The warmth of sentiment in emails, texts, and conversations eases the anxiety in me. The overwhelming notes summed up by "we're thinking of you and your family in your time of need" wrap me up like an infant snuggled tight in a blanket.

At seventeen, the uneventful, smooth and blissful life I have led until now leaves me with absolutely no way of knowing how to deal with what we face. I have no direct experience of death in the family, cannot recall serious illness nor even a terrible accident among those closest to me. Friends, teachers, my coach, and the strength that my mother shows, comfort me and help me to bear the agony. As Mum always says, "a problem shared is a problem halved".

The day finally arrives. I keep my mobile phone on and hold it tight as I sit in silence through every class, unable to focus on anything but news from the hospital. Eventually, the call brings relief: the operation has been a success. Mum is on the road to recovery, though with less intestine or bowel than she had before.I can breathe once more though a sense of unease is never far away. Mum stays in bed for the next week or so. I swim, study and visit her as much as I possibly can. Never one to lean back in her chair, she is used to being on the go, always has something to do, a dinner to cook or a parents' evening to attend. Now she is motionless, exhausted and in pain in her bed.

The 45-minute drive to the hospital to visit her is miserable. Coldplay's Fix You resonates in my head and ignites a firestorm of emotions in my heart. I'm suffocating in thoughts about the only thing I can think about. The lyrics and melody of Fix You engulf my soul. The song seems to be on the radio every time I get in the car. I just want my Mum back; I just want to fix her.

I take homework and meals into her ward so that I can sit and watch her sleep. "Darling, I'm too tired to talk. You should go home," she says, the pleading look she gives me convincing me to leave. Reality cuts like a knife.

"Ok. I love you," I choke, blinking back the tears. I walk out to the car, sit and cry like I have never cried before. Mum's words were few but painful for both of us. The love of a daughter for her mother runs deep. I would very happily have sat there all day and all night by her bedside in her room. Just to be in her presence, just to feel closer to her, just to be with her a few minutes longer.Driving home, Fix You is on again. It's raining.

Back home, I cry myself to sleep.The days pass and there are definite signs of progress; Mum begins to get bossy again. The operation removed some of her large intestine. Before she can be released, they have to make sure her digestive system still works and that she can eat something. The doctors insist on her having a 'farty party' before she can eat. Before they will give her any food she has to fart!The day I walk in on the party is the moment when I think that she is going to be ok. After being on an intravenous drip for nearly a week, she is being driven to distraction by her taste buds. She tackles the smallest omelette I have ever seen only to leave half of it on the plate because she is full. She tells me that she has never tasted anything as delicious in her life. Just goes to show how much we take things for granted. Through pain and struggles you're a friend indeed.

I hope we've helped you through your time in need.
Let troubles of insignificance back into your life
You've never stopped being the perfect mother and wife
This battle you fought you conquered you won
Just to let you know
I will always love you Mum.

CHAPTER 3

The Pain of What If

"Serious illness doesn't bother me long because I am too inhospitable a host"

— ALBERT SCHWIETZER

I arrive home from practice every day in November 2005, months after Mum's valiant efforts with a tiny omelette, to the ring of the phone and the sound of US college recruiters, American coaches. Information on dozens of universities rest in piles all over the house despite Mum's efforts to keep it all in one place. I have more schools to choose from than I have medals on the wall. The different criteria that Mum and I have decided I should look for in colleges are almost in the right order now, my favourite school at the top of the heap. Phone conversations, emails and a constant stream of facts and figures occupy my mind as I sort through the different advantages and disadvantages, prioritising, choosing as I go. My future rests on this decision.

It not only comes down to which school I will go to but, more importantly, whether I will give up the thing that has meant so much to me and is at the heart of all I do: swimming. In the last few months I have not been performing well by my standards. Since the age of ten, every aspect of my life has revolved around the pool. But now I am uncertain if I have reached my peak, unsure if I have what it takes to go further. Maybe I should just give up now?

If I choose a university in England I will definitely have to quit elite swimming. If I choose an American division-three school, such as Hawaii, I might not reach my full potential in the water or be a serious swimmer but will still swim for my scholarship and have fun with school. If I choose a division one school, such as Florida, I will place swimming at the very heart of my life's focus and my future plans.

Eventually, the basic choice is easy, my wish list clear: somewhere hot, a full scholarship and somewhere to swim and study with an equal opportunity to do well in both. Scraps of paper, square-lined and from the workbooks that Mum had left over from her days teaching mathematics, are covered in red-pen doodles, scribbles and words scurrying in all directions. The University of Florida and Hawaii both have an exotic ring to them. I had never dreamt of spending four years of my life in such places. The decision comes down to this: to be a serious swimmer or not to be one?

Dealing with coaches at a distance "across the pond" makes it a little easier for me to send out a block email to all the schools I will not attend know why I won't be coming. I call coach Martyn Wilby at the University of Florida, home to the Gators: my mind is made up and his university will have the mixed blessing of my company for the next four years.

An extremely fun December draws to a close. New Year is, as usual, the least planned night of the year. My last swimming training session of 2005 flies by in the morning. I complete every set as best I can and manage to swim my fastest practice times of the season. Dani Berry, a good friend of mine visiting from up north, sits watching enthusiastically in the lifeguards' chair as Graham Wardell, my coach, strolls along the poolside clasping his stopwatch. Like me, she can't wait to get going.

The afternoon is spent getting ready, the last of the hot water used on our showers, the hair straightener tested on full heat as we blast ourselves to a state of beauty. It's time to go and see Oli Jarvis and Laura Chase, fellow Portsmouth Northsea swimmers and two of my best friends, for the evening of the year, the night on which everyone expects to have the most fun they have had all year and bring in the new one on a high.

Music blasts through the car as we warm up for a night at Tiger Tiger. Pete Hall, another swimming friend, had got us all tickets to the 'party of the year' in one of the biggest clubs in Portsmouth. I arrive at Oli's house just as he is pulling out more alcohol than you'd find in a pub, in a manner of speaking. He has ditched his family New Year to come out and party with us. Kayleigh Bush, yet another member of the Portsmouth Northsea squad (all of whom I have a close bond with due to the countless hours we spend together), joins us. We've only bought four tickets to Tiger Tiger; how are we going to sneak an extra person in?

I drive us all to Portsmouth, we drink a little and wander around Gunwharf Quays attempting to scalp one last ticket to Tiger. Dani is only here for a week and I want her to have fun. Nothing doing: we can't find a last ticket anywhere. Now what?

It's almost 11pm, an hour to 2006 and we're stumped. Friendship and team spirit is strong in all of us. We decide, in solidarity with our one friend without a ticket, to head to Oli's house, the place where we know we'll find the most alcohol. And that's how 2005 draws to an end for the five of us, a sacrifice made, tipsy on more alcohol in one night than we had ever had in a month but happy too, embracing 2006 with the Jarvis family and hope in our hearts.

* * *

The New Year brings fresh hopes and dreams as I endure my first training session of the year. Back to the ache of work. The excruciating pain in the side of my stomach while I'm swimming only subsides when I flip-turn in the tightest ball at each wall. By nature, I don't complain much and have never taken a workout off even when sick. Skipping off is not an option in elite sport. Today is different. I have to get out and as I drive home after a very poor workout I feel like a pathetic complainer.

Tears subside on the way home but I'm confused, embarrassed. I can't understand: I always manage to swim through pain. I even swam on when I had tonsillitis. Did I really need to get out? Surely I could have finished the session?

I arrive home an hour earlier than Mum and Dad expect me, curl up in the smallest ball I can manage on the sofa and watch TV. I suffer in silence until my parents ask what's up. "I have this pain in my stomach, like a stitch, a cramp; I don't know what it is but just leave me. It'll get better. I don't want to talk about it." I sit here in fetal position until six o'clock as my parents and brother come and go. The pain is ever present.

"Do you need to go to the hospital?" Dad asks for the fifth time in the last hour. "I don't think so, I mean ... do you think I need to?" I don't really want to go but I have never felt this depth of pain. By eight o' clock I decide to go hospital after all, just to have it checked out. Dad drives me to Accident & Emergency down at the same hospital where Mum had her operation. We sit in the waiting room, conversation stilted.

A nurse gives me some pills to ease the pain. After what feels like an eternity I'm taken to a bed and they run some tests on me. A pretty little Chinese lady arrives to take blood. She reminds me very much of my school friend Vicki Hau and a conversation we had at school: each of my friends would grow up, learn a profession and never have to pay for anything because we would all give each other advice and help for free. Vicki, the smartest medic there ever was, would cure all sicknesses in the world, each illness felled by her genius.

Another two hours go by and Dad is irritated by the constant interruption of work calls. He's dealt with them all day and now they demand more of him at night too. I don't like people to wait on me. I tell him to go and that I can get a taxi home. He's having none of it and stays.

Some of the conversations I hear while sitting in bed alarm me: a doctor asks a young boy who has sliced his wrist if he's tried to kill himself. The patient dodges the question but the stories he tells about breaking up with his girlfriend suggests that suicide was what he had in mind. Little did I know how frequent these conversations would become in my life, a precursor to my experiences on the phone lines as a suicide counsellor a few years on in life.

A nurse returns to take more blood before I'm whisked off for an X-ray. The chap pushing the bed leaves me outside the X-ray room and goes through to check that they're expecting me. I feel nauseous. I haven't eaten all day, so no chance of throwing up, I think to myself. Inside the X-ray room I need a grey paper sick bowl: everything left in me comes out.

The painkillers don't agree with me, it turns out. Back in the A&E holding ward, the nurse tells me that they will have to keep me in overnight for observation because my blood count is a little abnormal. I am hooked up to a drip feed and face a weekend of 'nil-by-mouth', an experience that tells me one thing: I will never have it in me to be anorexic!

Having waited so long, Dad goes home alone while I wait for a bed to become available. An old lady arrives. She fell over in her bathroom because she forgot to use her stroller. At 100, she has a letter of congratulations from the Queen - and a daughter that she desperately wants to contact. This is the first time in a century of life that she has been admitted to hospital.

Sweet and frail, the old lady is full of wisdom but she's confused too. When the nurses start to examine her she struggles to fathom what they're up to. After an X-ray, she's told she has a fracture to her neck. A neck brace is fitted and she is left until they can find a room for me and a fracture doctor for her. It is 1am. Night nurses and on-call doctors have taken over from the day team and the relative importance of the fracture appears to have waned.

The old lady knows it and so the drama begins. "Cooey!" she cries. "This is rather uncomfortable. Excuse me, cooey . this is rather uncomfortable", she repeats in an extremely posh Queens-English accent, not once but many times, over and over. Nothing the nurse tells her appeases the centenarian. She's uncomfortable. So am I. I just want to sleep.

At last, they find me a room. Drugs numbing the pain, a drip feeding me, the white sheets, wires and the sound of beeping fade away as I slip into slumber feeling as though I'm plugged in to the rest of the room in some way.

The nurse wakes me at 7am and I manage to stay awake throughout the morning. Crosswords, magazines and drifting in and out of sleep fill the afternoon. It is just the start of a lengthy investigation into what might be wrong with me. Weeks of MRI scans follow as I go in and out of hospital. A camera is sunk down my throat at some stage so that doctors can take a deeper look. They're surprised by what they find in someone of my age, an ailment commonly associated with alcoholics or old ladies suffering from gall stones: pancreatitis.

It will be four months before I am able to swim again and my sports career looks as though it might come to a premature end. I'm determined not to let that happen, memories of a visit to Florida and the Gators urging me on down the path I've chosen to follow come what may. Dad and I had travelled out to the University of Florida's beautiful campus. Seeing the facilities, meeting the team, the coaches, the academic staff set my mind on overdrive. Everyone went out of their way to accommodate me. That is where I want to be, where I will be.

CHAPTER 4

To America - and Back

"It's not whether you get knocked down, it's whether you get up."

– VINCE LOMBARDI

Orlando Airport. I am sitting in a room with one man beside me who speaks no English and another who smells like moulding cheese mashed deep within a fat man's shoes. He smells so rotten that I think I am about to vomit after my long journey to a place and people I have only visited once before. Apprehension sets in with a vengeance.

I find myself searching frantically for confirmation that I have made the right choice. I have forgotten my I20 form, the document that belongs with the F1 visa you need to study in the United States. You cannot enter the country without it if you are arriving on a student visa. I'd realised just before boarding that I'd left the form behind but had called Mum, who in turn called Coach Wilby to arrange something in time for my arrival. I hadn't appreciated just how stressful it would turn out to be.

I'm sitting in a security room with no pictures on the walls, being treated to an intense interrogation process by a man whose strong accent I cannot place.

Blokes in uniforms march around. I feel very small sitting here on a rock-hard bench watched by judgmental eyes, twiddling my thumbs and longing for journey's end. I wonder if now might be a good time to get back on the plane and head back to where I came from.

Eventually, I get through the process with the correct papers. Mum probably found them in the safest place in our house, the place where anything valuable and anything important is always kept alongside a chocolate bar: her personal drawer. It was the first place I always looked when I craved chocolate. Ah, those purple wrappers on a Cadbury's milk chocolate bar: I would break a full layer off so that she might not realise that I'd stolen some. She always knew when I had. At some point, she kept only a Bounty bar or Fruit 'n Nut in that sacred drawer because she knew I hated coconut or any kind of nuts in my chocolate.

Now the drawer has come to my rescue once more as Mum and my coach-to-be pull out the stops. I drag my two huge pink suitcases across the airport, conscious that I probably smell as awful as I feel. Wilby is waiting for me, his olive-coloured skin evidence of a few years spent in the glorious Florida sunshine. I take my first official steps into the United States of America, visa in tow. New faces, new places, new weather, and new cars; my brain goes into overdrive once more.

I'm overwhelmed by my new environment. I'm excited. I cannot quite believe where this next phase of my journey has brought me to. I also feel anxious.

Wilby takes me to Target, the local superstore. By super I don't mean Asda or Tesco, I mean an 'everything you could ever need for anything, anytime, anywhere' kind of superstore. I need covers for my bed. Coach is a patient man.

We arrive at my dorm and struggle to lower my long, single bed down a notch of nuts and bolts on the frame designed to be adjusted for taste, comfort and people of different heights. My little dorm room consists of two beds, two desks, two dressers and two chairs, and connects through a bathroom to an identical room. The two rooms form part of a larger suite.

I meet my new roommate Kristen Beales. From Arlington, Virginia, she's on the cusp of a fine college career in the pool after a good club grounding back home. Her parents are with her. They're all been on a whirlwind tour of Gainesville as part of the process of helping Kristen to settle in. Their excitement and happiness at meeting me helps to settle my nerves but I feel a small pang of homesickness when I see Kristen kiss her parents goodbye. I wish my Mum and Dad could be here with me right now.

Beales is a tall skinny girl. Her awkwardness with new people is obvious and it will take a while for us to make friends.

* * *

With a semester under my belt, I am sitting in an auditorium filled with students eager to learn. The short man wearing glasses, suit and tie is balding. He looks extremely formal as he stands at the front of the classroom and explains a social psychological theory; he starts with an animated description of a letter sent home by a student to her parents:

Dear Mum,

Please sit down before you read this. I am sorry I have not been in touch for a while but I have been extremely busy here moving out of my dorm, after jumping out of the fourth storey [window] because someone left a candle burning and burnt down the building. I have moved in with my boyfriend of two weeks and am carrying his baby. We are engaged and extremely happy; due to be married within the next two months. I have a broken arm and am paralysed from the hips down after jumping out of the window. Finally I received a D in English and two F's in both Maths and French.

Please don't be too alarmed. I am doing really well, there was no fire, no boyfriend and no baby, I am not paralysed and both arms are healthy. However, I did get a D in English, an E in Maths and an F in French.

Hope you are fine and the dogs are well, did you and Dad get the new couch you wanted?

Love you, x

You could have heard a pin drop in the room. We sit in awe, wondering about the journey the professor is about to take us on. The audience is in the palm of his hand. I imagine how Mum would have reacted to such a letter. I see shock, disbelief, then relief as she sees the funny side. I draw up my own email to send home, one not far removed from the professor's mock. Mum's reply is not what I had expected: "That was not funny. We will Skype soon, I have something to tell you."

Two days of swim and school commitments go by before we can Skype. Saturday evening comes round and a long day ends with a fun night out downtown and a 2am return home. Sunday morning and Beales wakes for church. Normally, I might roll over and try to sleep on but today I realise that I have too much to do. I force myself out of bed, tidy the room, brush my teeth and turn the computer on. You get a lot done when you have a roommate who wakes early. The time difference between England and Florida makes Sunday morning the perfect time to call home. No school, no pressure. I sit in my room alone on the beanbag in the middle of the floor.

The news from home is almost as far from happy as it could be. All I can think is 'how could I have emailed that silly note before hearing this news, how could I have left it so long to call her?' I feel numb, paralysed.

I call my swim teammate Lauren Winter, my best friend from Australia and someone who understands me when I talk about what makes America different. She's had a late night too but doesn't hesitate to visit my room just to sit with me. I don't really know how to react, what to say, what to do.

The cancer is back.

I want to call coach Wilby, just to let him know that if I breakdown he will know why. I want to call Mum again. I need to call her back. It feels like there's an open wound in my heart and Mum is the only person who can sew it up - only she doesn't have a needle.

No one at UF knows me well enough, knows my family well enough, to know how I deal with emotional challenge. Only Mum knows what to say. Not even Lauren knows, although she does everything in her power to comfort me. I miss my friends at home. I want so badly to curl up in a little ball and pretend I am back on the holiday in Kos I enjoyed so much with my closest school friends after we'd passed our final exams when life was lived without a care in the world.

I walk in a daze through the dorms not knowing whether it is sunny or cloudy, not seeing the regular Sunday rush across the lawns outside the dorm, not hearing the summaries of epic adventures from the night before. I'm in a haze. All I can do is place one foot in front of the other. I try to rationalise my emotions; I try to fathom what she told me, what this means for me, for us, for our family.

I sign in to Facebook and start to write. I write to no one and everyone. I don't understand it, maybe someone else will. I write:

Being miles away is one thing, but when given bad news it makes it 10 times harder. I'm writing this note to say that my Mum is the most inspirational person I have ever known, she motivates me to get through the hard times as she is going through harder times. She is so tough that her strength of mind keeps her alive.

She is a fighter.

Overcoming cancer once shows strength in character, when faced with it a second time it creates another obstacle in her course, another crack in her path, but I truly believe in her, she will never give up and her love for me is eternal.

On Sunday, January 14, 2007, I received a phone call to say Mum had been diagnosed with cancer again and would start to undergo chemotherapy on Monday (today).

I don't want sympathy, I don't need sympathy, I am just putting this up to let you know; if I snap at anyone I am sorry. I feel lucky to have witnessed the strength in character once; we will get thru it again. We put on a brave face and look to tomorrow.

She is adamant that I stay here at UF, she tells me I have an amazing thing going here and I believe 100% that she is right. My motivation comes from her; the strength that she has found, used and shown, is something that I cannot put into words but I believe she has taught me one of the most powerful lessons without even meaning to:

Fight until you win, use all the strength within you to do the impossible. Never Give Up.

I love you Mum.

I post the note on my Facebook page for all to see. I allow my words to be seen by those who know me; I show my strengths by covering my weaknesses. I do not quite understand my reaction or why I have processed and dealt with it the way I have.

The distance between me and my family may explain some of it. The first time Mum told me about the cancer she was sitting next to me. I felt the warmth of her hug, drew energy from her strength. This time I'm alone and feel nothing but emptiness.

CHAPTER 5

Intensive Care

"Things can fall apart, or threaten to, for many reasons, and then there's got to be a leap of faith. Ultimately, when you are at the edge, you have to go forward or backward; if you go forward you have to jump together."

– YO-YO MA

October 19, 2007. Yesterday I was in Florida, today it's England.

"Pack your things, bring a suitcase back to the pool and we will book a flight as soon as one is available," head coach Gregg Troy said. "Come with me into my office, while Wilby calls and sorts out your flight." Coach Troy means well. He is a complex character, a man with caffeine highs and surprising bursts of excitement that sometimes break into constructive anger. He is the perfect mix for a coach leading a team of the size and talent on display at Florida.

I sit on the black leather sofa in his office, coach Troy on the swivel chair in front of me. He finishes a phone call with World 200m backstroke champion

Ryan Lochte and turns his attention to me. Silence. Men often don't know how to react when a woman breaks down in tears before them, I'm thinking. What follows does nothing to change my mind.

"I never know what to say in these situations," says coach Troy. "I'm just waiting for a call from my sister, she's in hospital too, nothing as severe but she's getting a hip replacement that went wrong - and got infected - sorted out." Deafening silence follows. He's doing his best to be sympathetic.

Wilby gets off the phone with Dad and coach Troy jumps in: "Grab Beales from the pool, get her to take you home on her scooter and pack and come back with your car, leave the scooter at home and we will take care of the car later, you'll come back and you'll be in scooter paradise!" A little confused by his train of thought, I run down to make arrangements with my wonderful, understanding roommate Beales.

I'm leaving my bankcards in the hands of my coach and missing practice to go and pack. Surreal.

After a few hours of packing and sorting out my school work with Tim Ayest, my academic advisor and the only person I know who can get a whole team of athletes through school, I eat no fewer than seven Krispy Kreme doughnuts. Maybe it was 12. We get underway. I'm about to fly home.

Beales sits next to me at Gainesville Regional Airport. She offers jokes, conversation and whatever else may stop me from thinking about what awaits me back home. On the way from Gainesville to Atlanta, Atlanta to London Gatwick, the flight music is unhelpful at a time when my emotions are raw. No matter how hard I try I cannot stop crying. I have never experienced such depth of emotion before. My childhood had known no such pain and all attempts at rationalisation fail me. I'm having an out-of-body experience. I'm looking at myself from outside. I feel sorrow for the crying girl who is me but I also feel detached from her experience, disconnected from her tears. I don't understand why she is crying so intently but I feel her pain. I see her in a plane, listening to the soundtrack of her tears, I see a mirror image of her and me reflecting back at me on the TV screen that serves as a barrier between agony and the understanding of it.

Dad meets me at London's Gatwick Airport. On the drive home we speak about America, my friends, my swimming and my school. It's easier that way. I can't handle the weight of the other thing right now. After I take a shower, we drive to the hospital. Preparing me for the worst, Dad explains that Mum looks as though she is withering away and that she is mostly asleep and will not hear me because of the many tubes she is attached to.

But she is ok, he assures me: this is just what intensive care is like. He calls on his own experience of days spent in an Intensive Treatment Unit recovering from Crohn's disease, another bowel ailment. He has first hand experience of a drug regime that leaves a patient in a peculiar state of half life, contentment brought on by switching off the body's awareness of itself.

I am prepared for the worst as we walk into the Intensive Treatment ward at St Richard's Hospital in Chichester. But Mum is awake, her eyes open. She is surprised and confused, happy and sad all in the same instant. I have never seen her like this. "Where am I? Why did this happen?" she asks as tears well and roll down her cheeks. "I'm sorry you had to come home," she says.

"Mum! I didn't have to come, I wanted to come," I reply assertively adopting the tone of caretaker, our roles reversed for the first time.

She is extremely confused. Her arms are pale and dry. She frowns every now and then as pain and confusion wash over her face in waves. I wonder if my presence drives home the stark reality of her situation. Is understanding somehow lost down the tubes that look like they are suffocating her?

Terror seems to have grabbed hold of her heart and tightened his grip. It is unbearable to witness. I look at my Dad and see the tears in his eyes too. A triangle of pain links all three of us. A tangled web of emotions governs me; fear, love, denial are all part of a cocktail of confusion that sits in the pit of my stomach and stifles any words that might have been spoken. Watching the strongest person I know and recognising the fear, upset and disorientation in her stirs the deepest of feelings within me. Alien feelings. I try to push them away, to deny their existence, while a small part of me says 'it's ok to be upset'.

The strength in my father as he stands holding her hand adds to the struggle within me. I want to take his pain, add it to mine and bury it deep inside me. I want it all to go away.

"Just one more," says Dad, holding her hand, "that's all you have to stay strong for." He almost whispers his words, forcing them out through a few cracks in his heart. "What do you mean one more?" Mum replies, a wave of confusion and turmoil passing over her face. She has still not understood why she is here in this bed and, most unsettling of all, why I am standing at her bedside. The last time she was awake I was in America pursuing our dream.

"One more operation," he says, "just so they can swoosh you out and put you back together." He explains the operation as though it is a water park slide or video game, trying his hardest to put a light spin on the heaviest moment of our lives.

We sit by her bedside for the next three hours. Small talk is awkward. I tell the tales of life in Florida, we exchange stories and jokes to lighten the mood as much as possible. In moments of silence my thoughts stray to sorrowful places where I wish they wouldn't wander. Tears are never far away and the aching ball at the back of my throat prevents me from talking. Time passes so slowly.

The nurses come and go. I feel secret gratitude for their interruption, the distraction an unspoken presence beyond their calling to care. Eventually, Mum needs rest. She needs us to leave, does not want to put anyone out, does not want to feel responsible for holding us up and has no energy to entertain us.

I remember the last time she asked me to leave and feel the familiar pin prick of hurt. I want to stay. There's nowhere else I'd rather be. I could just sit here while she sleeps. I am ok with it. But Mum needs to know that we are getting on with our lives as best we can.

On the way home, it feels odd to sit in the passenger seat after having become used to seeing a steering wheel on this side of the car. Dad takes a phone call from Wilby and passes me the phone.

"Hey babe," he starts.

"Hey."

"Y'alright?"

"Yeah, I'm good."

"Good, ok, so you got home ok?"

"Yeah, not a bad journey thanks." I keep my answers short so the strain in my voice is undetectable.

"You got a smile on your face?"

"Ha, yeah," I say, forcing one to take shape.

"Ok, we just finished with morning practice, and I thought I would give you a call. Just checking in on ya."

"Ok, thanks, I'll call you later, just driving home from the hospital now."

"Alright," he sighs. "Thinking of ya, call me if you need anything from me. Bye."

"Bye. Thanks Wilb". I keep my wall up as long as the call lasts. I don't want to impose my sorrow on him. Over the next few hours I try my hardest to keep the bricks in place but the cracks are starting to show.

I cook spaghetti bolognese for Dad, while he catches up on the rugby stories before the England Vs South Africa world cup final tomorrow. It's almost a normal day at home in England with him in front of the TV, only one glaringly obvious difference: the empty space where Mum would have been.

The cooking and homework serves as a distraction and I somehow push the images of Mum's torment to the back of my mind before we drive back to the hospital at 6pm for more small talk and emotional rollercoaster.

"What time is it?" she asks.

"6.15 in the evening," I reply.

"What day is it?" She wonders whether Saturday is close so that she can leave the Intensive Care Unit.

"Friday.""Why did it happen?" She asks for the second time today, her tone more lucid this time. "I want to be better."

The frustration in her and the overwhelming sense of drowning in this disease shows now more than ever. "When will I come home?" Tears follow. The two hospital visits have left me drained. I cannot fathom the level of exhaustion Dad must be feeling day in and day out.

Back home, I try to keep busy, finish more homework, read some more of Look me in the eye, a book about an autistic boy who struggles with social interaction. I fall asleep on the couch while Dad is watching TV, a mixture of jet lag and emotional devastation bowling me over.

I wake to hear my Dad saying: "I think you should go to bed."

In my room, I curl into the smallest ball and cry myself to sleep as my brain tries to work through the guilt I am starting to feel. I am not the one in pain. She is. How am I supposed to feel, how should I react? Confusion mauls me. I drift into unconsciousness.

"Darling it's time to wake up." Dad's slightly weathered voice soothes me. It's 9.30am, time to get up if I am to shake off jet lag. It's another chilly day in England, the kind of nippiness that calls for a winter coat and boots, a depth of cold that I haven't felt in a long while. Homework and catch-up phone calls with friends from England get me through the morning until the hospital update comes through: another successful operation.

Back on the ward, the atmosphere is different. Today she is asleep. Today I am stronger. Today I cry less.

"I don't like her like this," Dad announced. "I prefer it when she is awake, when I can talk to her." All I can do is nod. Mum lays peacefully on the hospital bed, the bag that collects her faeces attached to her and hidden under the blanket, though not well enough to conceal the truth about the disease that is slowly eating away at my mother like termites eat away at wood. I can't admit it out loud but I think I prefer her to be asleep, to be free of the fear in her eyes, the fear that saps the energy from her and leaves her weak.

Asleep, she looks calm and at peace. When she is awake, fear is ever present and I feel like I'm drowning in tears, the constriction in my throat unlike anything I had experienced. It feels like I'm suffocating.

Home again, I do more homework, sink myself into my book and then bring myself up to date with the latest swimming results online. I settle at the computer on the desk in front of the huge window looking out onto the garden. This is where I did my homework as a child, where I would sit with Mum towering over my shoulder, motivating and inspiring me to finish my tasks.

Dealing With It

The view of the tennis court, the flowerbeds, the tall black forest of trees towering over the fence and the frosty weather all feed my misery.

Reminders of my smooth-sailing childhood surround me as Dad catches up with the rugby. I wonder again: why us, why now?

A week later I return to Florida strengthened by a new sense of hope. Mum's recovery is slow but visible. My heart has been patched up. I have a heightened sense of purpose in life but where I appear to be stronger on the outside, I'm filled with doubt and insecurities deep inside.

CHAPTER
6

Mum's Death

"Death ends a life, not a relationship"

— MITCH ALBOM

"Nothing is ever really lost to us as long as we remember it"

— L.M. MONTGOMERY

A few months pass and I am jumping on a plane bound for home again. Yesterday, December 17, I swam the most amazing training set of my career; today I am waving goodbye. Eight hours of turbulence and I'm rushing through baggage collection into Dad's arms. We head straight to the hospital.

Mum has had a heavy dose of morphine and looks as high as she probably feels. She says "hi" and wants a hug and a kiss. I give her the scrapbook I have spent weeks preparing as her Christmas gift: memories, family pictures glued and pasted in a tome to cherish for the rest of our lives.

The weakness in Mum and the assisted wakefulness that goes with the drugs being administered make it impossible for her to get past the first page. "I'll look at it later," she says. Dad urges her to "look at it now" but I know there and then that the scrapbook is - and will only ever be - something for Dad and I to cherish in the future. She couldn't read it. I couldn't read it either, not without crying.

On the edge of experience, the smallest things live in the mind. I will later recall Mum playing with one of the buttons on my coat. She didn't have to say anything for me to know that she liked it; I knew she would, it was very her. The light brown vest-type jacket with no sleeves and lined with cream-coloured fake sheepskin was much calmer than the bright, vibrant colours she wore to work. Her sense of fashion had always been part of her huge personality, her choices a statement in themselves. Although you could see her coming from a mile off, her taste in home comforts was subtler: like the brown and cream jacket.

Some of the memories I will come to treasure most are the things she did that helped shape a part of me, made me aware of myself and reminded me of the pride she had in me: reasons to be proud of myself.

I often recall one of the moments that will live with me always: we were at Swindon pool for a competition and I was standing getting ready for a race (I can't recall which race nor precisely how old I was) when Mum said: "People like you because you are a nice person. You have all these friends because you are nice to people and because you are kind they want to be around you."

I take pride in not judging people; I take pride in putting others before myself, even if they don't always deserve it. Mum's words that day would shape and sculpt me; they settled at my core, remain a part of my fabric and will grow and evolve with me throughout my life.

Watching soaps and movies, I had always wondered why the hospital-ised were made up to look as they did. Now, in this room of care and rest, I know that most directors have it spot on: Mum's eyes are black-rimmed, her skin awfully yellow, even a hint of green about it. There is no makeup in this hospital. None is required. This is real life, a life ebbing away. Doctors can do no more, we're told. No more operations, no more physical inva-sions. From now on it is palliative care, given in a local hospice, St. Wilfrid's in Chichester.

The hospice staff arrive early to collect Mum. Aunty Margaret, who has been staying at home with Dad for a while now, hugs him and me as we all set off. We're in tears as we follow the van that transports Mum. She is extremely confused as we try to settle her in her new room overlooking the garden. The sun streams in. She looks more tanned than me. Had she known it, she would have smiled at the thought. She had always worshipped the sun.

We talk to her as she drifts in and out of consciousness. Later in the day, we lower the morphine dose a touch and she is able to whisper words such as "I love you". Aunty Margaret and I will always believe that she also said "I can see Mummy". My aunt had told me that their Mum had died at the exact same age - and from cancer too, although a different type. There can be no question in my mind that my grandmother came to meet her daughter that day and take her on.

Sitting here in this unfamiliar room with my family around me I realise that I am, quite possibly, the luckiest person alive to have a mother as strong as she is, a father who deals with everything that seems weighed down by the impossible and a brother who trusts me enough to cry on my shoulder. My emotions are raw, intense.

I turn to Dad and ask: "How did you propose to her?"

"Yes, I proposed to her."

"No, how did you?"

"Well, it was right after I came out of hospital. You know the windmill up on Halnaker Hill. Well, we walked, yes walked - ha! - up that hill and I collapsed at the top, sitting back against the windmill overlooking the countryside to the sea ... I brought out the ring."

"How did you get the ring?" my brother asks. Peter is very bright. Always one to pick up on the tiniest of details, he sees the small things that directors get wrong in movies, he always thinks outside the box, always questions the most obvious yet complex things.

"Erm, I don't remember, honestly. I don't even know where I got it from."

"If you were in hospital how did you get the ring?" I ask.

"I really don't know," said Dad. As the conversation moves on, a substantial part of my parents' relationship becomes a little clearer to us but the detail remains hazy. It must wait for another day.

"Did you fight over boyfriends?" I ask Aunty Margaret.

"No."

"Different tastes?"

"Well, she didn't have a boyfriend until she went to university. And I think she only had two at Uni too."

"Daddy and who?"

"Dave Groom," Dad pipes up.

"Oh, I see - a little bitter about that one?"

The questions and light humour soothe my emotions. It is important, somehow, to get to know her past before she begins her new journey. Time flies faster than it ever does on any given "normal" day, the ebb and flow of it all bringing to the surface feelings that I have never known before.

Words cannot describe the rawness of being this day. The last words Mum says to me are: "I love you very muchly". I tell her I love her too and then I say goodbye.

Dad tells me that I should go home and sleep after a long day of travelling, no sleep, no food, an emotional roller-coaster of a ride. The waiting, the worrying could go on for days, he says. Dad tells Mum that Peter and I are leaving. I will long remember the pained look on her face. I think I hear her say "wait" - but we leave because Dad thinks it is for the best.

Back home, we set up camp in the living room. The dogs sleep there too: they know something is up. I truly believe that they understand the gravity of it all, even if they don't really know what it all means. Peter brings all the blankets down from upstairs and I cook dinner for us, another spaghetti bolognese. I only realise how hungry I am when I sit down to eat.

That night, I sleep no more than three hours, waking to the sound of my brother's breathing on the floor beside me or to the pawing of a dog. I ham just drifting off again when Dad arrives home a little before 8am.

Mum has gone. She passed away peacefully at 6.30am. It's the 19th of December. I embrace Dad. I cry but I'm confused too: why was I not as upset as I thought I would be? I hug Dad because I think he needs it more than I do. Peter waits. He needs a hug from Dad too.

I wander down the hall dazed by the events of the early morning. The corridor is out of focus. I'm numb. I have no control over what just happened. In the bathroom I see the blurry edges of an aerial photo of our house. I want something to happen. Some drama. Does this moment not deserve drama? I plunge my fingers down my throat; I need to rid my body of this toxic feeling. Nothing. I look in the mirror and think: WHAT THE HELL AM I DOING? It clicks. I am out of control. I need to control something but this isn't the way. Nothing comes up. I can't even do this right, can't even make myself vomit.

The week that follows is filled with letting family and friends know what has happened. Everyone I can think of manages to get in touch in the week leading up to the funeral. The support, the comfort, the kind words are more appreciated than many will ever know. I could not have asked for more from anyone.

If the memories of that week will later become blurred, the day of the funeral will remain with me forever. I push back my leaving date by a day so we can have the funeral on the 28th. Come the moment, I am ready to tell the world what an amazing woman my mother was. To give the eulogy at the funeral was the least I could do to tell all who knew her what a towering presence and influence she has been, and remains, in my life.

My final assignment in my speech class earlier that autumn semester was the eulogy of a person "either living or dead". I forget whom I spoke about but the exercise prepared me a little for the real eulogy I am about to deliver. It gave me the strength to know that I could stand in front of the people gathered here to celebrate Mum's life and speak in my developing transatlantic accent (not quite English and not quite American).

At the crematorium, a lady comes up to the hurst that I'd chosen with Dad and Peter and tells us that we will have to wait for the party before us because the deceased is a young man and the gathering therefore bigger. I mishear her and understand that she put the cause of the wait down to the dead person being so big that he would take longer to burn. We make a little light humour of it. Dad and Aunty Margaret laugh but Peter is unimpressed and all my attempts to lighten his mood fall flat.

For Mum:
Closer to me now than you will ever be,
Your spirit will be forever in me.
The beginning of a journey in my heart, strength and love
With your guidance from above
In life you touched us all, now you strengthen us more
Strengthen our endeavours; more than ever before.
Fighting the battle you fought right to the end,
Inspiring became a common trend.
The peace in your departure will satisfy us
You never did make a fuss
When your Mummy came to meet you;
She came to guide you through.
I will always know where to find you
To say you're not around is untrue
You will always be in our hearts, the stars and the atmosphere.
Your love and spirit will be forever here.

CHAPTER 7

January and The Hobbit

"No doubt exists that all women are crazy; it's only a question of degree."

– W.C. FIELDS

January dawns. A new year and hopefully one that will bring much more positive news than the last did.

My Mum's dad passed away just a week after his daughter. He was very ill and I believe that once he knew that his little girl was waiting with her Mum, his wife, he was able to let go and leave this world for the next. It comforts me to believe they are together, to believe that they're looking down on, or living through me. My Grandad was an interesting and glorious man who, with passion and ease, told me stories of the war and his life. I remember with great fondness those days when we would sit together in our conservatory looking out at the garden, his wisdom filling my ears.

Sadly, his death and my mourning for him are overshadowed by the grief I feel for Mum's passing. That's not to say that I never think about him but those thoughts are often sunk deep beneath the all-consuming memories of Mum.

The beginning of 2008 provides a stepping-stone to a new outlook on life; there's lots to be done and little time in which to do it all. The urgency within me makes me feel somehow as if my own death is imminent, that life is running away from me at a hot pace. Each and every day I ask, "how should I act"; "how should I feel about all the events that happened last year"? I come to a simple conclusion: I will carry on with life just as Mum would have wanted. Back to work in the pool, head held high, emotions in check.

January in Florida starts with a cook-off between my house and the class above us, Kelsey and Laurabeth, both wonderful teammates and practised bakers and chefs, against Beales and I, neither of us so well-practiced in the kitchen.

Our Menu:
Homemade bread
Starter - Melon Salad
Main - Coq au Vin
Dessert - White Chocolate Torte

Their Menu*:*
Black Bean Salsa and Deviled Eggs
Starter - Summer Salad
Main - Fried Chicken, Mash Potatoes and Biscuits
Dessert - Chocolate Bundt Cake

It's good to be busy, to be distracted for a while from the weight of recent events that prey on my mind almost every waking minute.

I call Dad and make a note in my diary: called Dad, told him how amazing Beales' new skills are, cooking, building a desk! Was nice to catch up, never really spoke to Dad about everyesay things before, was normally Mum, was refreshing to talk.

I read Mum's diary and made a note in mine: it is strange reading, she was younger than me but still a lot of the same problems, this guy Nick became interested in her- and so she didn't want him anymore!!!

Her diary is so important to me. I feel that I have a deeper understanding of the complexities of a life she was never able to talk to me about.

While it comforts me, it pains me too. Memory is crystal clear, tangible, in touch, sound, smell. I see her in slow motion in my mind's eye. The images haunt me. Pain, confusion, fear, desperation, all etched on her face in the last moments we ever shared together. I see her frail, delicate hands as she reaches for me and plays with the button on my jacket; she hands back the Christmas present I give to her, card unread, gift unopened because she is just too tired. I also see the fight in her and grasp hold of the only thing I have left: I am so very proud of this woman who gave birth to me, loved and nurtured me, played a spectacular role as Mum and taught me so very much.

Some things we have to learn for ourselves. Trying to make sense of relationships, from within them or from afar is not for the impatient.

My housemates call him the Hobbit. He's the centre of most of my endeavours right now: in fact, he's become an obsession. He's the boy I sit all alone by my phone and wait for a message or phone call from; I'm depressed, angry and confused if I don't hear from him for a couple of days but elated and excited when I do; he's the boy my roommates hate. I realise all of this and yet my obsession grows with each visit, each encounter.

I put everything I have into a relationship that isn't really even a relationship; make it out to be something huge, like he's the love of my life. I'd met him before my Mum passed away and we went on a few dates. We went for gelato the Sunday before I left for England and he had blueberry, which in his word was "Intense!"

I sent him a message via Facebook before I returned to Florida:

Hey, This is another loaded msg; and for that I am sorry.

I am also apologizing for the previous pathetic attempt of a fbook msg; and I also believe I need to apologize for the appalling explanation I gave, for said pathetic attempt of a fbook msg, on Sunday; which I will unduly put down to my inability to deal with conflict (conflict is definitely not one of my greatest attributes).

You may be wondering why I feel the need to send you this msg because it may sound like female emotional s**tty babble that no guy cares about & would run as fast as they possibly could from (which I wouldn't blame you if you did!)

However, I am sending you this msg from England; after my Mum passed away peacefully this morning and I believe that I should leave no stone unturned, and say what I really mean to say and not just tell you what is easiest for me to tell you.

(If you stop reading now because this is more intense than your blueberry ice cream I understand completely; right now my heart aches and I would understand if this is too much emotion for you in one msg)

So here is the explanation I should have given on Sunday:

Previous guys in my life have been a**holes, and by a**holes I don't mean that they didn't call when they were meant to, I mean actual a**holes - I will not go into why or how, as I do not think you really want or need to know. But experience tells me that every single guy is a complete a**hole.

However, you are not an a**hole. This in itself makes me uncomfortable, in a nice way, but uncomfortable nevertheless; because I have never experienced what you are making me experience, and inexperience for me is quite possibly the bane of my life. Because of it my defense mechanisms appear in full force, a wall goes up and fbook msgs get sent that should not. I have learned a lot about myself over the time I have known you - for that I thank you - whether you realise it or not you have taught me feelings, respect and how NOT to be when around (or not around, more to the point) someone you like. I apparently look for the asshole in everyone ... you have taught me, so far, it is not always there.

As you obviously know by now, I like you: however, right now I do not know if these are true feelings, or if I am replacing something I feel like I am losing, or if I'm trying to create an ideal man out of someone who I do not know well enough: because you make it easy for me to do so.

Just writing this msg has relieved me somewhat; and even if you didn't read it, it has brought me peace of mind.

Merry Christmas Hobbit,

Happy New Year,

And I hope that knowing you have this effect on girls has assured you that you definitely are not just an ordinary guy!

The Hobbit's reply came in three parts and I still had no idea where I stood.

2:34am Jan 6th

I probably should've read this before I left on break...i'll do it now.

2:39am Jan 6th

I like your wording it's very intellectual or whatever.

Your mom passed away? Your family has my prayers.

This message as a whole was rather flattering. Thanks.

Also in the beginning of it where you're being introverted and beating yourself up. Don't do that.

2:40am Jan 6th

Sorry for a few separate messages. I hope you're doing Ok with all this. I'm tired - I just got back into town today.

Ok, I'm going to bed. Have a splendid day tomorrow.

Two days pass and I get another call from Hobbit. He leaves a message this time, so I text him and tell him I will call him after practice. I am really nervous, I think I'm really starting to like him. Practice, after a long team meeting, is pretty rough. In the step set, in which pressure mounts the further we get, I swim really well at the start - and get slower and slower with each passing round, the opposite of what's called for! Still, I'm not slower than last year, so I figure that must be good! The post-training massage is wonderful. I go for dinner, head home and tell Beales what I'm about to do. I finally pluck up the courage to call him. I ask him if he wants to come round. There is a tedious silence before he sort of says yes. I can see on my phone that Julianne is calling, the beeping a secondary irritation as I listen to Hobbit making every excuse as to why he can't come round right now. I tell him to do his errands then come over if he has time.

Beales is listening. When I put the phone down, she freaks out. What, she asks, was I intending to do with him when he got here. I'm so clueless when it comes to dating. In fact, was it even a date? Ahhhh! Now I'm freaking out. I make sure the room is tidy.

A while later, he calls: he is on his way. He makes a pitstop, calls again and gets directions, staying on the line until he arrives, a DVD of Seinfeld in tow. We put it on, he eats his sandwich, talks about Christmas. It's kind of awkward, yet not. Steph Proud comes out of her room and there's an easy introduction. Beales follows - and I feel really glad they're both here.

Hobbit talks to them while touching my legs every now and then. I tell myself not to read into it, to just be natural. Let it be. Easier said than done. Beales takes a sleeping pill and Hobbit thinks she's weird. My roommates go off to bed, leaving me and the Hobbit to watch Seinfeld. I no longer feel awkward but still don't really know what to say.

Whenever I feel him look at me I pretend I'm engrossed in the show, although I really want to look at him and kiss him. He needs the bathroom so I tell him to go to mine. I'm not sure how I feel about listening to him pee so I busy myself with my iPod to be distracted. He emerges, gives me a hug and says he needs to go. As he is about to leave he turns back to ask me: "Are you ok?"

"Yeah?" I reply, sounding a tough confused.

"Well, you sent me that message," he answers, I think to myself 'Must stop sending Facebook messages!'

"My Mum and my Grandad both passed away." We talk a little about what happened and he says he's praying for me. I ask what he thought about my message. He doesn't answer and I feel confused. He leaves and I have no idea how I feel about him.The next morning, I have to go and sort out something related to Mum's pension: I don't want money, I don't need it. I just want her back. The guy handling the paperwork keeps asking me questions I don't know the answer to. It's unpleasant. On the way home, I call in on Coach Troy and Wilby so that I can fax the papers back from their office. Coach Troy tells me I can eat chocolate, in moderation . but I'll take it!

Just as well. Back home, I grab some books and head off to sit by Lake Alice. Tears are never far away in this place. I think about Mum and allow myself some space to grieve. I think of her deliberately, allow myself to remember. I feel selfish about crying but think that I am entitled to cry every now and again. Aren't I? It's just not fair that she is not here; there's so much I need to tell her. I question and argue with myself, the devil's advocate inside me on the go from morning til night. I feel like I'm going mad. People have it worse than me. I feel so sad, and yet so happy to be alive.

The next day, I keep thinking about Hobbit. I feel like I want to sit him down and tell him exactly how I feel. But I don't even know how I feel! I think that I may be trying to create a relationship to fill my void; anyone would do yet he is the one here and now. I want to tell him that I have read enough books, seen enough movies to know that people in my situation try and grab hold of someone, to replace what they have lost.

The last thing I want is to make him feel obliged to speak to me, to see me. I have a distorted image of him: I see him as someone who would be there to cuddle every night even though he has only served that purpose once, maybe twice. Should I tell him? Will there be a right time to tell him? Maybe I will meet someone else soon.

Right now, I'm falling in love with a fantasy. I'm inventing stories. If he wants me in his life, he will call. My mind is made up: I must not, under any circumstance, call, Facebook, poke, text or email him.

CHAPTER 8

Dr Death & Mum's 50th

"Quiet is peace. Tranquility. Quiet is turning down the volume knob on life. Silence is pushing the off button. Shutting it down. All of it."

– KHALED HOSSEINI

I get in line for a speech on campus by Dr Jack Kevorkian, one of 40,000 people ready to consider a very controversial topic. Commonly known as "Dr Death", he's a pathologist, euthanasia activist, painter, author, composer and instrumentalist. He champions the right of terminal patients to die through physician-assisted suicide, claiming to have helped 130 people leave the world that way and says, "dying is not a crime". It has all got him into a lot of trouble.

Today, he speaks on peoples' rights, lack of understanding over what rights we have and how we don't stand up for them: the Ninth Amendment. He speaks a little about euthanasia, although due to the conditions of his parole he is not allowed to talk in detail on the subject of euthanasia. He talks too about politics, about the need not to condone the war in Iraq, not to class those involved as heroes, about classing as a hero the officer who stands up and says he will not go to war.

He speaks of "sanctuary", advocates a system in which criminals choose their punishment according to the wishes of the families of victims. I don't know if I necessarily agree with him but his words are interesting and thought-provoking. He defends a charge of having taken the life of someone who was not terminally ill by saying that he euthanised a person suffering from Alzheimer's because she didn't want to lose her mind and she didn't want to live anymore.

I think about Mum in that context. I wish I could remember her more clearly from a time before cancer, before chemo, before morphine. Maybe it is ok to kill someone with Alzheimer's because if you have a parent who doesn't know who you are, that will be the last memory you have of him or her. Am I just satisfying my own self-serving memories, I wonder. All these thoughts may serve me well one day, I conclude.

My mind flicks a page: no call from Hobbit today - a good thing, perhaps.

I call Dad, have a wise conversation with him, tell him about "Dr Death" and listen to him explain the Ninth Amendment: "The enumeration in the Constitution, of certain rights, shall not be construed to deny or disparage others retained by the people." In other words, if the majority of the public decides that one of the written constitutions is wrong, then the power of the people can rule against it and deny that right as laid out in the constitution. The Ninth Amendment, in essence, says that the rights that are specifically laid out in the Constitution can't be used to supersede the ones that people are inherently born with in the United States, the right to die included. Just 21 words long, the amendment struck Dr Kevorkian when he first read it in jail. "The most powerful, the most precious thing you have . is the Ninth Amendment," he said.

Meanwhile, I need to wean myself off constant Facebook and phone checking to see if Hobbit called. Why am I so obsessed? I need to stop replacing Mum with Hobbit. There is no comparison. Stalking him on Facebook has allowed him to introduce me to Mark Knopfler, politics, reading, and has given me a severe thirst for knowledge. I need to accept that this "relationship" is a one-sided story. Hope is wonderful, false hope apt to lead to fantasy and delusion that takes over body, mind and soul.

Learning from false hope, taking the knowledge of this newfound love of learning is what I can gain from my experience. It is what I intend to take from this friendship/acquaintance/crush - but I'm not ready to move on just yet.

The Hobbit is the centre of my world as I go on my fourth or fifth date with him. We decide on dinner but when he arrives he has other plans: he wants his jacket back from one of his friends who lives 'out in the goonies', so we should go there. Fair enough, I think. He's met my housemates, I'll meet his friends.

It's pleasant sitting in the company of total strangers. I want to touch him, to hug him, to hold his hand. I feel an almost unbearable tension between us but I don't want to show it in front of all these people I have just met. I don't feel comfortable with making a move. I figure I should wait to see if he does. He doesn't.

We drive home around 11.30pm with a third person in the car. He drops me off first and I just walk away and go inside. I'm comfortable with how I feel, no regrets. He goes home tomorrow. So be it. I do really like him and I was more myself with him today in the company of others. I'm still unsure of how I feel. Let it be.

Two days later, Tuesday, January 22, 2008, is the day Mum would have turned 50. I make her a card and write:

To my dearest mother on her birthday,
Just a little something to say;
I love you forever and ever,
In any kind of weather.
Happy 50th Birthday; smile and be blessed,
For you are finally at rest.
In my heart you will always remain,
Wherever you are have a glass of champagne.

I buy flowers before practice and go and sit by the lake, still, quiet, peaceful for a while. The sunlight glistens through the trees as the turtles and alligators wade around in the waters below. The university is a distant backdrop to this place of solitude and calm. The soft sounds of wildlife hum in my ears as the rays of light engulf me in a warm light. I feel serene. I can think here. I can heal here. After training, Wilby and Troy make me cry when they tell me that it will be an emotional day and that I can do what I want with it.

I can see the vase and four stems of lilies intended for Mum as I connect to Dad through Skype. We make arrangements for his next visit, which coincides with the Southern Eastern Conference College Championships. The team leaves for the competition next Monday.

I make some notes: Beales to get senior gifts for the girls on the team. No call from Hobbit. Screw him. He calls as I'm on my way home from shopping. He can't do dinner. He lost his car, he says. So what, I tell him, I'm already going to dinner with my friends, Steph, Beales, Kimmie and Colleen.

I find myself giving him the benefit of the doubt. When he says I can call round later on my way home, I say "ok". We end up having a really nice evening: we cuddle while watching What About Bob and laugh a lot. It gets too late to leave. He says I can stay and we cuddle some more. We kiss. That's as far as it goes. I doze in my jeans all night long, deep sleep hard to come by.

I really like him and not in the way I liked boyfriends such as Philip and Jamie back home when we were young. That was just physical. I spoke a lot more to Philip than I did to Jamie but even then it still wasn't a friendship; there was no deep emotional connection and feelings were based on looks. To be able to lay in bed with someone and not feel compelled to get physical is an unbelievable feeling. We lay down beside each other, hold hands; that alone feels more intimate, our fingers entwined, than anything I shared with Philip. Hobbit plays with my hair. My feelings for him stretch to liking him an awful lot. Is it love?

The next day, all day long, I long to call him, long for him to hold me again. I feel giddy. He sends me a video of Tenacious D. I figure he will call me when he's ready. I don't want to put pressure on him and scare him away because what we had last night is something so very much better than anything I can recall from my past.

In a reflective state, my search for understanding leads me to a book, Motherless Daughters by Hope Edelman, once owned by my mother. She has scribbled and underlined passages and phrases that scream at me from the avalanche of advice.

"Early parent loss makes a child more vulnerable to feelings of abandonment and worthlessness, which makes her both fear and desire relationships as an adult"

"When a motherless woman attaches herself to a romantic partner so quickly and so completely, her attraction derives almost exclusively from what she hopes he can give to her"

"The tendency to look for nurturing in relationships with partners who can't possibly meet our needs and the awareness that early loss has shaped, toughened and even freed us, helping us make changes and decisions we might not have otherwise made"

I go and sit by the lake again and read Mum's diary. The moonlight flickers through the trees onto the lake as the stars glisten in the night sky. Happy 50th Birthday Mum, I love you.

CHAPTER 9

Team is a Family

"I am a member of a team and I rely on the team, I defer to it and sacrifice for it, because the team, not the individual, is the ultimate champion."

— MIA HAMM

A deep sense of longing for what I will never have again follows me into a new week. On the way to the College Championships in Tuscaloosa, I chat to friends, listen to music, keep a smile on my face and feel as though I'm ready to race. At least in the water, things go well: I win the 100 and retain the 200 yard backstroke crown. My times are good, dividends starting to roll from all the work I've put in.The US college system offers swimmers and athletes in a range of sports a chance to hone themselves in the most competitive environment in the world. Whichever way you turn, there's a world-class act, individual or whole squad in your path.

Each race session is packed with multiple events for each of us, while screaming for teammates is part of the theatre of team effort. The bond between us is akin to family: the undeniable connection you create with complete strangers through sport resonates deeply and makes you care just as much about how others perform as how you fare yourself. This stage either makes you tough or tells you whether you're suited for world-class waters and a shot at a big podium one day.

College swimming teaches me to take racing and competition in my stride, the fun of it, the spike in the challenge and the frequency of racing all apt to make you a worthy rival for anyone out there.

A couple of weeks on from SECs, we travel to Ohio State for the National Collegiate Amateur Athletics Championships. The Big One. Reputations on the line. Programme funding on the line too. Being a member of the NCAA dictates that you can't accept private funding and race prizes, which would make you a "pro", professional athlete. Most of those who come this way, it seems to me, agree: any downside is outweighed by huge positives.

That said, the day before racing I still don't feel like I am at NCAAs: the atmosphere on the team is not at all pumped up. In fact, we're all completely subdued, even the coaches are very calm.

We make our way to the pool in the morning, our session followed by a lazy day in the hotel. I watch Atonement with my roommate and fall asleep halfway through. I snore my way through the rest of the film, my amused teammate in the bed next to me tells me when I wake up.

Liz Goldson, a former teammate from Florida, has come up to watch the meet. I really enjoy seeing her and not only because she sneaks me a chocolate brownie when the disapproving eyes of the coaches are not watching. Race day dawns and it's really intense from go. I feel exhausted after the opening morning session: having to do three races really takes it out of me and I need to take a nap in between sessions. I rest my head back on the pillow and stare up at the photos we have pinned to the door. The parents have put together posters for each member of the NCAA team and Dad has sent me some snaps of Mum and my wonderful brother. There are also some up there of me and girlfriends from home. My eye is drawn to Mum's image. I feel the stab of grief in my heart, sadness balanced out by the inspiration, motivation and sheer joy I get from knowing she is always with me. It's good to see her face again.

On the way back to the pool for finals, we drive past a cemetery and then a cancer survivors' unit. Each time we pass that way, I feel my emotions welling up and have to look away. I hide in the sound coming through my headphones. Electro-music pumps me up for finals and keeps sad thoughts at bay.

All things considered, the meet goes really well. I win both the 100 and 200 yards backstroke, the latter for the second straight year. In the 100, I clock a time of 51.78, Hailey DeGolia, of Arizona, the only other under 52, on 51.89. I win the 200, my time, 1:50.70 comfortably ahead of Kateryna Zubkova, of Indiana, second in 1:53.17. My teammates Steph Proud and Leah Retrum take fourth and fifth.

Looking around at the people who have supported me and the coaches who have prepared me I have a deep sense of belonging. My 200 time says a lot about the work I've put in and the progress I've made in readiness for Olympic year: I'm 2.26sec faster than I was when I won a year ago over 200. That's good.

I race in the consolation final of the 200 yards medley too and we end the meet in sixth place, our best result in four seasons. Arizona, Auburn and Stanford are out ahead at a competition that features a lot of people who will go on to excel at the Olympic Games, such as Rebecca Soni, of Southern California, on 59.19sec in the 100yds breaststroke. She will win the Olympic 200m title later in the year. Right now, that achievement remains a target.

One of mine is to make it to China too - by qualifying for the Britain team at Olympic trials looming ever larger on the horizon.

Chapter 10

Olympic Trials & Time To Say Goodbye

"The future belongs to those who believe in the beauty of their dreams"

— ELEANOR ROOSEVELT

Tuesday, April Fool's Day, 2008: an appropriate day for what unfolds at Britain's topsy-turvy Olympic trials this morning. I'm in the water for a wake-up swim because qualification heats are being held in the evening, finals in the morning, the exact opposite of what we're used to. We're practicing for what those who get to the Games will face in Beijing, where the schedule has been turned on its head because the timing of morning finals suits the American broadcaster NBC and its domestic audience and advertisers.

In finals this morning, Mel Marshall and James Goddard, two of the biggest names in the sport in Britain missed their events because they didn't check into the pre-race call room in time. "Really?!" I think to myself, my mind squared against the mindset and other things in Britain that I was glad to have left behind when I moved out to Florida.

I spend much of the day resting in my room, popping out for lunch before heading back down to the pool for my first test in heats. It's good to be relaxed at such moments and know that you're enjoying what you do and the company of those you meet. Perhaps the biggest thing I will take away from this sport when I finish my career is not the races I race and the competitions I win but the people and the community or family I have made that make it all worthwhile.

It's refreshing to have Aunty Margaret and Hugh, her husband, here to watch. Their presence and chatting to swimmers on poolside helps me to avoid the stress and anxiety I feel in an environment I ran away from when I left for Florida.

Stress takes another form too this year. In February, Speedo introduced a new suit called the LZR Racer. half of the bodysuit is made of polyurethane panels. It's the first time that non-textile apparel has been allowed in the sport and the whole issue is on a collision course with controversy that will end in a ban on such garments just two years down the road. The first thing we all notice is the time it takes to squeeze into the tiny, black, almost Catwoman-like suits: you have to stretch and peel them on, the tightness, or compression, part of the explanation for faster times all round. And the trick is to get the suit on without getting a nail caught. One false move and the material rips.

I dance my way into the suit long before my race and sit down next to another competitor, Sarah Owen, a young girl I used to train with in Portsmouth. I feel relaxed and stretch and strut about a bit before walking out to the start of what might be an Olympic campaign if all goes well. I could hardly have a better start: 59.89sec in the heats of the 100m backstroke. That performance makes me the first British woman ever to swim inside the minute. A British record in my first swim. It tells me that the work I've put in is about to pay dividends.

Making the team was not the main purpose of this trip home from Florida. A world record would have put immense pressure on me yet both coach Wilby and coach Troy believe that I can be the first woman to break 59sec. So 59.89, while good and granting me a ticket to the Games, is not the end of the line. It is, however, enough to make my spirits bounce and feel that I'm on the cusp of something amazing. Even so, the constant striving for perfection that is ingrained deep within most competitive athletes anchors me in a positive way. It's unhelpful to get ahead of yourself.

The swim is the best I've ever done - and it hurt a lot too. After interviews in the mixed zone where we meet the media across a barrier after racing, I enjoy a pleasant dinner with the family. Back at the hotel, I brush off that empty feeling I get when I think of Mum and call my teammate Liz Goldson over in Florida and have a chat. My mind buzzing with thought, sleep is hard to come but I drift off eventually.

In the morning I feel fine. It's going to be a good day. Warm-up for the goes smoothly and I'm smiling as I stand behind the blocks waiting for the whistle that tells us we can jump in and get ready for the start of the 100m final. There is a strange heartbeat-like sound over the tannoy as British Swimming officials attempt to silence the crowd for the start. Many in this final may be asking themselves if the sound if that of their own thudding hearts. I'm relaxed and ready to race. I feel like I have nothing to lose after all that's happened, although there is always a touch of apprehension when everything is on the line. I race: 59.90, just 0.01sec slower than the record I set in the heats last night. Good enough for gold and my first selection to a Britain Olympic team. I'm happy but I don't feel extreme emotion, at least not straight away.

In the mixed zone reporters pay far more attention to Lizzie Simmonds. She's 16 and just done a best time of 1min 00.66, inside the target time. She'll be there alongside me in Beijing. I'm glad for her. She seems bright and I think we'll hit it off.

The truth sinks in when the lights die down, the media fades away and I find a moment of solitude in which to reflect: I've just made the Olympics. I'm going to live the dream! As I make my way to the podium Dad throws down a picture of Mum so that I can wear it while I'm getting my medal. I pin it to the pocket of my tracksuit top but the media doesn't notice and no one asks me about it; this moment is for us, for her.

There are sobering moments too, I go for a drugs test and it takes me an hour to pee. I am stranded in a basement room below the swimming pool with tiled walls and cold enough to chill the mood. When finally think I can relieve myself I'm taken to an even smaller room where I must choose sample bottles to pour my urine into. I sit on the wooden stool at a cheap metal table as a complete stranger watches me pee in a container, handles my urine sample and places it in the bottles bound for a laboratory.

After a long wait, I'm free to go and have lunch up in the gallery at the Ponds Forge pool with Margaret and Hugh, Dad and Peter. That's followed by shopping with Dad via a quick change stop at the hotel. I treat myself to new shoes, buy a bear (from one of my favourite shops in the world: Build-a-Bear) for Wilby, then head back to Dad's room to answer some congratulatory Facebook messages and speak to BBC Southern Counties Radio.

When I get back to the pool, Wilby's happy, with my performance and the bear. He gives me availability forms to fill in for the meets and tour the Britain team will be attending on the way to Beijing. I also have to update my official biography.

I see Chris Walker, a close friend of mine, in the scoreboard room working on the technical side of the timing board at the Sheffield pool. He was one of the four relay boys from Fareham Nomads Swimming Club I used to see a lot of. Each one of them - Peter Hall, Nick Barber, Chris and the boy who meant much to me and will remain just Philip in this journey of mine - have shone rays of sunlight on my life and have long been my cheerleaders in the pool.

After following the heats at the pool this evening, I watch Desperate Housewives. It's the empathy episode and the empathy within me clasps tight around my heart as I relate so strongly to the plot. It's the cancer episode and I cry when one of the characters says that she watched her Dad die. A warmth spreads over me when she says she thinks he can still see her, memories of my mother come rushing back and engulf me with warmth. It's been a long and exhausting day. I feel like I could sleep for a month.

The hotel fire alarm sounds at 4.30am. Everyone is out on the street for half an hour. I'm lucky enough to manage some more sleep before I go to the pool to watch the morning finals. Others who were up at 4.30 just don't bother to go back to sleep.

After finals Dad calls to say he has a problem. It turns out to be that tickets for the Games in Beijing are hard to come by. He is struggling with the notion of booking expensive travel to the other side of the world, flights, hotels and all, when he's not sure he'll even get in to the pool to see the action. It is one of the stresses and strains faced by the families of Olympic athletes who have put in years of support, care, love and money but often get little or no help when it comes to making sure they can be there to watch the big moment that all the dedication was aimed at. My father has devoted so much love, time, energy and resource to my career. It hurts me to see him so frustrated.

Friday evening, brings the heats of the 200m backstroke. It's been a boring day, the monotony of lazing around in hotel rooms starting to grate. I'm feeling a little flat, the emotional high of the 100m having sapped my energy. I'm already longing to get back to Gainesville, truth be told. I've not had much experience racing 200m in a long-course pool (Olympic, 50m long) and my heats swim is all over the place. I don't think it would have been possible to put together a more clumsy 200. That said, I'm in the shape of my life: the time on the clock beams back a big personal best. The last time I'd swum a serious 200m long-course I went 2mins 12.93sec back at the 2005 national championships. Today I crack 2mins 10 for the first time with a 2:09.71. Lizzie claims lane four for the final in 2:08.79, and my Florida teammate Steph Proud goes 2:10.46 just behind me.

Go Gators!

The next morning, I'm still feeling flat and unmotivated. It's not until I walk out behind my blocks for the final that I have a smile on my face and suddenly feel ready to race. Performance sport is a fragile thing sometimes. Habits and attitudes formed over long periods of time can kick in just at the right moment if ingrained during years of dedication and discipline. That almost explains how it is possible to ask an athlete half an hour before a big race how they're feeling, hear them reply "rubbish" and then watch them get in and do a best time. Regardless of how you feel on the cusp of a single race, you've prepared for the moment of truth for years.

I go 2:09.71 in the final, Lizzie wins in 2:08.99 and Steph misses out in 2:11.10. I feel sad for her but I'm also happy that I got through. I'm glad it's all over too. The Olympic trials are done. After lunch at the hotel I pack some stuff ready for travel and take a nap. I just want to fly home to Gainesville and climb into my own bed and be with my friends in Florida. I want to draw a line and put the pressure behind me. Don't misunderstand me: I'm grateful to have my family and friends here in Britain, great to have people I care for and who care for me to share a meal and go shopping with. And that's just what I do. It's a good way to put the trials behind me; the job is done, the tension fades away.

Come the evening, I go to dinner with one of my friends and see some of the other swimmers out and about. Some of us go on to a few clubs and enjoy a drink or two. Sunday brings the team parade at the pool and an Olympic squad photo before I leave for Aunty Margaret's place and another world.

I will long recall the sound. I hear the quiet chink of metal handles on wood over the gentle hum of the car engine as we drive down the winding roads towards the cemetery in Otley, Yorkshire, on a mournful Monday morning. Mum is in my heart, her ashes on my lap, enclosed and sealed. This will be her final resting place.

As we pass through the narrow gates of the cemetery, a lump builds in the back of my throat. Snow has settled on the hills around us and the gravestones at our feet. All is still. We're struck by the majesty of the setting, the sheer beauty of it all biting at our emotions.

The Payne vault stands before us. I ask about the names engraved in our family history, a slight distraction from the moment we're about to face. The two caskets containing the ashes of Mum and Grandad are lowered down into their final resting place. The people from the cemetery grant us some time to stand at the grave, I think of Mum and come to terms with a reality as cold as the day around us. The silence between all five of us here this day set-tles to the bone. I pull my parka hood close to my head. We're lost in thought and feeling so deep that I can no longer feel the chill air as tears pour down my face.

I can't look down any more. I stare into the distance and take comfort in the spectacular Yorkshire hills, white as far as the eye can see this day but so often on previous visits luscious and green. She will be here with her Mum and Dad in this stunning landscape season come, season go. Dad comes over and hugs me.

"I wish she knew you'd made it," he said. "She knows," I think to myself as Dad tells Peter and I: "It's time to go". Gently, he turns me around and walks me back to the car, leaving Peter behind with Margaret and Hugh as they say their farewells to Grandad and Mum.

Back at the house, Peter and I mess around like we're 10 again. It's time to say goodbye again. Tears well up in Margaret's eyes as we wave to her from the car bound for Manchester, her silvery blonde hair blowing in the wind of a day that will live with us until we live no more.

I say farewell to the rest of the family in Manchester, rent a movie, order room service in the hotel and take a call from a local paper in the Portsmouth area. I find the reporter really frustrating, his questions stupid and long winded, he drags out the interview so much longer than other reporters. It doesn't go well and I'm glad to say goodbye.

The next morning, after checking into the flight home to Florida, I face some questions that make me feel like I'm a terrorist or something. The cus-toms woman asks when I'm returning and doesn't seem to get it that I have a visa to stay in the United States. I buy £25 worth of chocolate and on the plane find myself sitting next to a lady called Janice who asks me to sign her book. It feels really weird; making the Games is certainly not something that qualifies me as being "famous" enough to sign autographs!

Beales picks me up at the airport in Gainesville. I have barely unpacked before I'm thrown straight back into the start of summer here in the Sunshine State. With a couple of days to spare before I have to get back into swimming and classes, I have a high time with the people who've become central to my life. A group of us head to Orlando for the weekend. We take in theme parks, roller-coasters, water slides; dancing; get home in the early hours, get to bed at 4.30am; watch Sex and the City videos; attend as many parties as we can.

I've got through most of the list of "how to let your hair down" before Dad calls to ask if I got home ok! The trials already seem like a distant memory. I'm in a very different world. At a party held by the gymnastics department, eve-ryone is getting naked, both literally in some cases and also in terms of the

American expression that conveys a sense of letting it all hang out and not being shy to express yourself.I remain vigilant and conscious of what's going on around me. One of my friends later thinks she avoided getting date raped. She was convinced that her drink had been spiked. It seems we all got out of there just in time. By the time I arrive home it's 4:40am.

Routine, discipline, dedication, the road to the Olympics drag me back down to Earth the next day.

CHAPTER 11

Summer and Psychology

"A problem shared is a problem halved."

— PROVERB (AND LESLEY SPOFFORTH)

Finding the courage and strength to surrender to people, to finally admit that I need help may well have been tougher than actually walking through the door of the psychologist's consulting room. Beales walks into my room and catches me crying, not for the first time. She suggests that I might benefit from speaking to someone other than her. Her wisdom proves to be a turning point; it's the first time I'm able to submit. I need to give in, I cannot live a moment longer as I have been living. However determined I am to achieve my goal and get to a better place, I somehow lack the strength to stem the tears.

I spend my time moping, each day I cry but should anyone ask I am unable to explain precisely why. I simply sit and see my life as if through a lens. It is as if I'm in a movie, each move I make, each thought I have played out to the sounds of my sobbing. I'm going through the motions in the pool.

When Beales walks in, I'm sitting in my room on my bed, staring into space. Every sad song about losing someone wails from my playlist: Norah Jones, Westlife, James Blunt and others in a mournful medley to match my mood. One song transcends them all: Fields of Gold by Eva Cassidy. It is the song that accompanies cancer charity adverts. It always made me cry, even before Mum was struck down by cancer.

My first session with psychologist Wayne Griffin is hard. I arrive not knowing what to expect. The paperwork I have to fill out shows several issues that I can work with him on. Not only am I feeling pretty depressed but one of the consequences of that is that I'm struggling to get along with roommates and to communicate with family. Top of my list, however, is 'dealing with loss'.

Before Wayne came along, if anyone asked me how I was doing the answer had always been 'good, Mum has given me the strength to carry on with life, and she will always be with me'. It was the perfect auto-pilot response, one that suggested that it was a pleasure for me to carry her memory with me and gain strength from that wherever I went. There was truth in that but deep sorrow too. I still struggle to explain to myself and cope with the fact that I burst into tears each time I think of Mum.

Some weeks ago, before agreeing to see Wayne, I arrived home from dinner, locked myself in my room and cried. In truth, I wanted someone to walk in, I wanted a cuddle from Beales but just could not bring myself to ask. I escaped the house through the door in my room that allows me to leave unseen and unheard. I wandered to the lake, the darkness of the shadows between the sporadic streetlights in keeping with the charred edges of my heart. The empty streets felt like a canvas for the loneliness and isolation I felt, my desperation mirrored in the silence of the world around me.

The tears never cease as I drift towards the lake. I imagined walking out into the road, being hit by a car. I wonder whether anyone would realise that I was missing if I didn't turn up anywhere. I contemplate staying out all-night to try to get my head straight. I sit by the lake and cry some more. I just need to escape this life and this emptiness, free myself of the dead weight in a heart heavy enough to sink me to the bottom of the lake and keep me there.

All I want is an easy out. If I could only get away from it all, things would be easier, wouldn't they? Actually, everything is getting harder. I think of calling Liz, my roommate who has gone home to New York for the summer; I think of calling home; I think of calling Beales. But I cannot bring myself to dial. I just feel so very alone, frozen, a thick fog of emotion clouding my judgment.

* * *

Wayne's sheet asks "have you ever thought about suicide?" I answer 'no'. It is an answer that I will stick to throughout. It seems that I have two parts to my brain, one a contradiction of the other and one more dominant than the other.

Mindset one: yes, I am in a huge, dark hole with no one to help me out, and the one person who could is no longer on this Earth, and yes, if I had jumped out in front of that car everything would have stopped, no further need to focus on swimming, no need to seek answers, no need to analyse why I'm feeling as I do.

Mindset two: if you listen to number one, then all those who are inspired by your strength, all the people who admire who you are and what you are dealing with and how you are dealing with it will be let down, all those people who are there for you, constantly, unconditionally even though you keep them at bay will wonder what they did wrong and what they could have done to have prevented tragedy.

The second mindset always wins: I cannot accept defeat, I won't give in to the easy escape. Both sides of my brain work overtime but there is only ever one winner. Mindset one is overruled by two. So, yes, it has crossed my mind, but no, I have not contemplated it. That is my rationale in answering 'No' to the suicide question.

Wayne asks me many a question but much of what we speak about lives only for that moment. Only small fragments will be retained in long-term memory. I can tell you that he told me it was ok to cry. He asks me why I don't cry in front of people. I reply: "I don't want people to think of me as being weak, so when I cry, I cry in the water, into my goggles, or back in my room and if someone asks what's wrong, I brush it off and won't let them listen because that's my role, it is who I am: I'm the listener. If someone is sad, I'm the one who listens and talks and tries to help. It is not Ok for me to be the one crying."

Crying is the body's way of healing, says Wayne. He asks me what my friends would do if they saw me crying, what would I feel about that. I say: "They would sit and listen and I would be sad but I guess I would be comforted to know I'm not alone." Through the talks I have with Wayne, he manages to convince me, or allow a part of me to convince myself, that it is ok to cry and it is ok to let people know that I'm sad.

Much later I will come to realise that I am actually being selfish by not letting people in. My academic advisor Tim Ayest once told me: "I am very similar to you, I don't like being a burden on others and I won't cry in front of them. But someone told me once 'You're being selfish, you are depriving others of the one thing you hold most dear to you. You like to listen to others' problems, you like to help: others like to help too and you are being an egocentric pig'. After that was said to me I think I allowed people to help a little more."

He is right: I am being selfish. I will never be someone who always asks for help but I will come to develop the skill of allowing myself to do so every once in a while. Along the way of learning, if someone asks me why I am crying, I am often lost for explanation when it comes to knowing precisely what triggers the tears at any particular moment.

Depression engulfs me like quicksand sinking a soul. The more I feel it suffocate me, the more I seem to have to feel it. I almost want to feel it. The more I stay in my room and lock myself away the harder it is to escape back to the 'normal' world. The harder it is to laugh and giggle, the easier it is to cry. If I didn't have to get out of bed to swim I would never leave my room. If I could hide away for the rest of my life and never interact with people again, I'd be quite satisfied. I'd just keep crying and listening to the sad songs on my playlist.

Wayne asks what reply I give when people ask what's wrong. "I say nothing and walk away, I don't feel like there is anything wrong, although there clearly is … I have nothing to say, I don't know what to say," I tell him. "Just tell people that you're missing your Mum," he says, pointing out the pure truth of it. It is precisely why I am crying.

I manage to do as he thinks best. I manage to speak the truth to teammates, like the Fraser brothers Shaune and Brett and to Mike Joyce, the next time they see me cry. They say they're sorry and leave it at that. It makes everything so much easier: I'm no longer putting a strain on all my relationships, I'm able to get on with things without my friends taking any of it personally. Ease sets in my mind as I no longer endure the painful expression of helplessness in their eyes. Talking to Wayne makes my life a lot easier, if only because the behaviour he recommends provides a way of talking to people about Mum. He keeps telling me not to refer to death as an "it" but refer to my mother and say that she has passed away, to speak the truth: my Mum is dead.

It is hard to do but dropping the "it" in favour of "Mum's death" makes me realise that the strength that I had shown to the outside world until summer 2008 was just a wall; a wall of denial.

When people talk about the stages of grief and speak of denial, they don't always mean that it didn't happen, just that those left behind deny to themselves that it has affected them. I managed to win SECs, NCAAs and make the Olympic Games; therefore I must be fine. I had been able to continue on through life as if nothing had changed: "it" had not and would not affect me. Of course, "it" did affect me, deeply.

Anger, bargaining, depression and acceptance are the other stages of grief, I'm told. Anger is not something that I believe I am capable of showing, though there will be those who take me to the brink during my days as a swimmer.

I am depressed as I spill my emotions out onto this page, purging my depression in black and white. Bargaining I am not sure about, while acceptance is something I feel some days but not others. Wayne thinks that these stages are not a point-by-point, 1-to-5-stage process. The journey is more cyclical, he believes, the pattern apt to repeat itself each time something reminds me of Mum: a birthday, an anniversary, something someone says, a picture, a place. The cycle cannot be learnt, cannot be rehearsed because each time round the sequence will alter. The bottom line: it is ok to cry.

Many days pass before it is ok for me to smile again or at least until the smiling is truly meant, truly intended for the people around me and the people that know I'm seeing a psychologist and are there to prop me up. It is a while before I'm able to tell people that I'm working on it with Wayne, that I've sought professional help. When I do tell people, I realise what a good thing it is to be seeing someone: I'm feeling better about everything and the experience is helping me to talk about Mum.

Bradley Ally, a fellow Olympic swimmer and Gator, takes me to dinner. We sit and talk sincerely to each other for about two hours. He pays before I even realise it. His genuine care touches a part of my heart that I had considered cracked and crushed. He allows me space to become human again. He somehow knows what an emotional toll all of this is for me. Dinner, surprisingly, is not at all demanding or awkward. I feel like I've made a good friend this evening. We share our thoughts on the Olympics and talk through our emotions on other stuff. It makes for a very pleasant evening and I'm glad I've been to dinner with my teammate.

I feel a little more confident about talking through my feelings since Wayne and dinner with Bradley proved to me that people can and do listen and care.

CHAPTER 12

The Start Of Healing Back In Britain

"If there is no struggle, there is no progress."

— FREDERICK DOUGLASS

I pack just a few bags. I'll be away from the place I now call home for months on end. I feel like the world is spinning but I am standing still. Time to go. It is actually happening at last. Reality dawns: the Olympic journey begins.

I stumble from my bedroom to the front door, dragging my half empty luggage behind me. I'll be getting a whole lot of kit when I reach England. Maybe the bags need to have space so I might have a place to store the mountain of emotions weighing heavily on my shoulders.

I don't really know how to say goodbye properly. Is there a proper way to say farewell when you know you'll be back soon enough? Perhaps it's just the upheaval of it all but my emotions are on edge. I'm anxious, fearful, sorrowful and excited. I don't know quite what to expect as I leave my newly acquired family for a temporary life back in England, the country that I left behind.

I'm unsure of the friendships I had, may still have and could yet develop on the British team.

Walking into the living room, I yell "bye guys". Beales comes over and hugs me, then Omar Pinzon, a Colombian Olympian, each squeeze representing a mass of people behind me, people who have supported every step I have taken and will be behind me at every turn on the voyage that I'm about to embark on. It's a journey that I've dreamt about for as long as I can remember.

The first hurdle is a struggle. After a pretty uneventful flight, Coach Wilby and I land in the North of England. The beautiful, rolling hills and lush green landscape make it feel good to be home again, though Wilby's driving skills on the 'wrong' side of the road make for a precarious ride. His stick-shift skills were lost somewhere between his college years in Kentucky and his coaching years in Florida. We somehow find our way to the pool in Liverpool before jetlag, mourning and lack of sunshine hit me harder than expected.

Wilby is also feeling under the weather. His "man 'flu", a cold to us womenfolk, death's door to men, rears its ugly head. When he picks me up from the student accommodation where we're staying his head looks fit to explode, his face is warped with tension. He looks like he needs to sleep for a month. Not the best way to take the next stepping stone to the Olympics.

At the ASA Championships, prelims (primary qualification rounds) are swum at night in preparation for the Games in China. The first prelim out of the way, I'm back in bed. I'm confined to what can only be described as an up-market prison cell, a very small hard bed, uncomfortable and cramped, a small desk and a built-in shower/toilet in the corner of the room. It's 2am and I'm still awake. Depression comes creeping; slowly at first, then in a rush before it settles deep in my gut.

I am exhausted, I am overwhelmed and I just want to sleep. I see flashbacks of my mother. Slow tears precede a waterfall of emotion. I see vivid images of the tanned, skinny woman sitting on her hospital bed, life ebbing away from her. I see the scene as if looking through one of those funfair mirrors that goes on forever; with each passing image Mum gets progressively worse, moves ever closer to the last memory I have of her on her deathbed.

The sterile smell of hospitals pervades this temporary prison cell. A vision of Mum stares into my eyes, fear and love etched on her face. I'm engulfed in grief and pain. The image keeping me from sleep is not that of the person who taught me how to drive, or the woman who sat with me while I learnt integrals in higher-level maths. It is that of an unknown, lifeless, terrified woman.

I feel crazy. I talk to myself, argue with myself, beat myself up for feeling like this. "Just go to sleep Gemma, seriously, you have no right to be feeling like this. People are in poverty; people have lost both parents, even whole families. Stop." I feel as though I am watching myself in a movie, again! I hear the soundtrack to my misery and feel the emotions of the girl on the screen; the now almost familiar out-of-body experience, I'm detached, remote. I wonder how often I am going to feel this pain and how many times I will see the images before I make the link: this is real life. My life. This is happening to me. To her. My mother. To us. My family.

My alarm goes off, my eyes are puffy and so tightly closed that this alien place with its rock-hard bed are a blur. Am I really here?

Next thing I know we're on the way to the pool again, Wilby's driving skills improving, his medicine bag refuelled. I swim the 50m backstroke, finish third and then head for lunch with Dad. Although not too many words are exchanged, especially about the difficult night I've endured, I take comfort in his company, in his silence.

The feeling is short-lived. The meeting room at the pool in Liverpool is full of faces I know, names I remember and people I feel I ought to know well. I feel out of place. Everyone else knows each other, everyone knows me by name and face but no one really knows who I am.

Sitting among rows of fellow Britain swimmers, I listen to speeches about making sure our 'whereabouts' forms are correctly filled out in accordance with anti-doping rules, about what could go wrong in China, what to prepare ourselves for. I'm still exhausted. They hand out gifts. To my utmost surprise, not only am I given a Nintendo DS with a game to load in readiness for the battle against boredom in the Athletes' Village in China, but I also get a pair of Bose headphones to block out any unwelcome noise when we're relaxing in Beijing.

Here in Liverpool, I'm still uncomfortable but I loosen up a little as events unfold. Some of those I have been friends with in the past are breaking down a couple of my self-protection barriers and that helps me to relax. Just as well: ballroom dancing is next on the agenda. Pairing up, we all find a space and learn a few steps. Michael Rock, butterfly swimmer and law student, is my partner. He's a little shorter than me. Dancing never was my strong suit! Enjoying the klutzy, non-athletic ballroom dance, sabotaging every last ounce of dignity will live with us for years to come and helps us to bond as an Olympic team. One day "Rocky" will race against the great Michael Phelps and beat him, just once. It won't be when the heat is on but he'll have something to tell the grandchildren.

Back at the pool for evening heats, the 100m freestyle feels smooth. The big event for me, the 200m backstroke, feels horrendous. I have dinner with

Dad then it's back to bed again. I manage an hour of broken sleep, waking constantly to the same pain in the pit of my stomach. I need her. How am I supposed to survive in a totally unknown environment in Beijing in this state? My emotions are too deep to fathom. Sad. Upset. Depressed. I cannot, and do not, swim fast in this state. I am tired, exhausted in fact - and I miss her and I miss Florida.

A flash of hope. Aunty Margaret is coming tomorrow. Hopefully, I will be able to talk with her. Prone on the padded wooden slab that passes for a bed, I watch eleven o'clock come and go, then twelve, then one ...

Breakfast is uncomfortable, Wilby knows something isn't right, I can read it all over his face but for some reason it is impossible for me to articulate what is going through my mind, what I'm feeling.

I find some comfort in sharing my emotions with John Atkinson, one of the head coaches on my European junior team a few years back, a coach who my Dad has kept in touch with while I've been away in the States. I guess it is easier for me to talk to him because I don't know him as well. Perhaps I don't need to keep anything from him to protect myself, don't need to keep deeper emotions in check with someone who is not that close. I can allow the cement wall that protects my heart to subside even if only for a few minutes.

Wilby, like most people who know me, sees me as a strength, a rock, someone whose emotions are buried beneath the surface but someone who can deal with the tough times, the way I want people close to me to see me. John hasn't seen that side of me, hasn't seen how I've been coping since Mum's death and I'm able to relay some of the pain that's weighing me down. Sucking the energy from me.

He introduces me to Duncan Richards, the Olympic team psychologist, a kind man with a gentle voice and empathetic eyes. I have a meeting scheduled with him for later.

Margaret is here but we cannot seem to find the time to talk privately. Each time I see her there are lots of people around and so I just talk about the counselling, skim the surface, keep emotions, thoughts and words simple. Simple enough to keep the tears back; too much talk and I will cry, open the floodgates once again and wonder if I might never be able to stop.

Speaking to an absolute stranger about everything somehow releases the tension in me. Once I start talking to Duncan, it's as though a steam train is escaping from my mouth. Choo-Choo! The passengers are pain, hurt, anger and anguish, depression, anxiety, each leaving the station in turn. Understanding dawns: it is time to conquer them all.

"If your Mum was still here today, what would she say to you?" Duncan asks me gently. I look at him as I consider my feelings, tears falling down my cheek. I notice the change immediately: I have not been able to sit and cry so openly in front of anyone without feeling a deep sense of unease.

"Erm. I don't know, erm .. I guess, erm .". Words, sayings and conversations fill my mind. Not a sound falls from my lips. Conversations between a daughter and a mother, the love, the bond so strong, easy to feel, impossible to articulate in the presence of a stranger.

After a long silence, Duncan asks: "As in right now, if you were having a conversation with Lesley and not me, what words would pass between you? I want you to actually sound out what you would say to her and what she would say to you."

Feeling as though I've been stabbed, I reply: "Hi Mum. I miss you so much, I feel like I need you here to help me conquer this."

"And how would she reply?" Duncan continues calmly, letting me cry and letting me feel the pain right here, right now, with him, not in my own time but in real time.

"Hi darling, It's not the end of the world.. A problem halved is a problem shared.. Tomorrow's another day.. Worse things happen in the world - and get on with it." She had spoken similar words often enough when the going got tough. She had been my rock. My memory of conversations in which she came to my rescue are crystal clear. My words are disjointed and rambling, but Duncan nods, listens, understands.

He then hits a nerve with the follow-up. "You probably have something you need to do to move on. Something for closure that perhaps you haven't thought about or perhaps you have forced yourself not to think about." I wonder if I need to go back to her grave. We didn't spend much time in those beautiful green hills, the majestic landscape that I see as a place of peace in which she is happy.

It just feels as though grieving and denial have no place in my life right now: events whizz past me so fast and I can do everything without the intensity of feelings. I have been fighting off grief, putting it off until after China but the truth is that the frustration of dealing with not dealing with it has heightened my grief, ripped at my emotion all the more.

From this moment in the room with Duncan, I set my mind to letting it happen, going with the flow, doing things that may be a little uncomfortable but somehow help the healing.

Integrating slowly with the team is settling and a mountain lifts from my shoulders. I begin to feel more comfortable and wonder if the negative feedback I get from Dad and Wilby about the team here in Britain has taken away from the strength I have gained from the team back home in Florida. The Gators are 100% behind me, supporting every success and every failure.

I have placed it on such a high pedestal in my mind that this British swimming team, one I left behind two years ago, might never be able to match up.

This was the British swimming team that cast me aside, forgetting my existence, the people who cannot put aside pride to communicate with my coaches in Florida: going overseas has set me in a different club, one that gets no funding and is not seen as part of the home-made success. That contributes to a negative perception when I see the words **British Swimming**.

Sunday rolls around and the final of the 100m backstroke feels smoother than the prelims, even after I'd fallen asleep on the poolside before the race!

Dad drives me from Liverpool to Loughborough, the British Swimming headquarters and the national team debrief and bonding camp that will take place there. We chat, nothing deep, and listen to the sounds of British radio. When it's time to say goodbye, I wave to him. Julia Beckett, an Olympic teammate, calls out from the corridor behind me: "Give him a hug?!" Too late. Dad was already climbing into his car.

I settle in with Kate Haywood, Julia Beckett and Caitlin McClatchey in their house and I finally realise that I can actually fit in with these people. All three, plus their respective boyfriends, sit down next to me to watch television. I feel so much better than I had in Liverpool. I'm finally able to get to know my teammates in a way that would not be possible as long as I put up a barrier labelled "I hate British Swimming".

Enjoying genuine conversation and getting to know my teammates on an individual basis overrides any negative feelings that remain about the British set-up.

Kit day arrives! Wilby drives me to pick up what turns out to be an overwhelming amount of Adidas branded kit, the Olympic logo printed on each and every piece of clothing and luggage. Two blue and red luggage bags full of red, white and blue t-shirts, sweatpants, hoodies, rain jackets and swimsuits to take to Japan, where our holding camp will be staged, and China with me. Officials guide me through a fitting room of Olympic clothes and apparel of every kind hung on racks. It feels like Christmas and my birthday all rolled into one. A lady is there to tailor my suit for the opening ceremony. I'm reminded of Mum making my prom' dress. I still don't know how happy I feel doing all of this without her. For that very reason, the level of thrill among my teammates seems to be a step up from mine.

On the way home, I find the courage to tell my coach: "That was hard, Wilby, she would have been two steps behind me in everything I am doing," but the words hang in the air. Neither of us knows what to say next.

Back at the swimmers' house, Julia and I cook dinner together. Her gentleness and subtle inquisitive approach allows me to let my guard down a little. Her open, genuine and beautiful personality matches her face. Her manner, bubbly disposition and attention to detail make it easier to discuss things that I would previously not have wanted to talk openly about.

Answering simple questions about how I deal with the loss of a parent or how much I think about her settles me into a subtle rhythm of acceptance. Talking with Julia and Kate makes living with these newfound friends easier. Their search for understanding is uncomfortable for me but in talking through my emotions, I no longer face them alone. I don't know if everyone knows about Mum's death, nor do I want anyone to tiptoe around conversation, nor feel like certain questions or subjects are out of bounds. I don't want people not to ask.

I am at my most uncomfortable when others are uncomfortable around me once they hear that I've lost my Mum.

CHAPTER 13

On The Way To China

"We can endure much more than we think we can; all human experience testifies to that. All we need to do is learn not to be afraid of pain. Grit your teeth and let it hurt. Don't deny it, don't be overwhelmed by it. It will not last forever. One day, the pain will be gone and you will still be there."

— HAROLD KUSHNER

I'm going home for the very first time since she died, since the funeral. It's a daunting step in my grieving process and I'm expecting vivid memories to haunt me. Come the moment I'm given a couple of days break away from our Team Britain base in Loughborough, things are not as bad as I feared. Walking through the door I'd walked through countless times before, I'm greeted by the dogs, barking madly, absolutely no room for sadness, their tails wagging frantically with excitement. The beautiful black and white collie-crossed spaniels, two dogs filled with energy and personality. We play fetch outside in the garden so familiar to me since my early childhood. Jaffa always catches the tennis ball, Apple is not interested at all, never was, her nose where her pride is, high in the air, as I imagine her thinking 'such a childish game!'

Empty cupboards, full loads of laundry. Mum is not here to do it for me now but I'm here and my memories of this place are full of happiness. I don't feel the depth of sorrow that I have often felt when wondering about life, Dad, my brother, here at home in Britain. I'm so far away in Florida it's hard to imagine that life has continued without me, happy memories have continued despite our tragedy. I walk the dogs, jokingly but with a hint of serious I tell Dad he is fat, watch two movies; and play fetch in between sleepy cuddles with the dogs. I feel better than I thought I was going to on this first visit home since she left us: I shed a tear before bed but manage a long, satisfying sleep.

My Granny, my Dad's Mum, lives next door. She sits in her conservatory as life floats by. I watch her as she wonders why the dogs are roaming free in the garden when there's no one home. She spots me and comes out to chat. She's happy to see me as we stand on the invisible divide between her garden and ours. As I take in the beauty and colour of the flowerbeds, I recall the countless conversations and venting sessions that Mum had after brief encounters with the little old lady standing next to me.

In a voice shaky with age and sadness, she tells me: "It's sad that Lesley isn't here." I nod, tears welling. She sees what I see: "Lesley would have liked this, she would be here and watching you play with the dogs, so proud of you."

The space between her words and my silence is uncomfortable. I cannot get a sound past the ball of sorrow constricting my throat; tears sting, sear. It is as if a jug of water has been poured into the glass of my eye.

Eventually, Granny asks: "How is Dad doing do you think?" She's concerned for her child but is unable to ask him herself, unable to harness the bond between a mother and a son and really understand where he is emotionally, even though they live next door to each other.

"Ok," I reply. "Ok ... he tells me when he's not. He's grieving, I think." Our chat is imbued with sadness. I try to cling to the things of here and now. The Olympic motto for Beijing comes to mind.

One World, One Dream ... One woman, and a whole lot of grief, I think to myself.The short break at home over, I am back in Loughborough, flat, emotionless, unable once more to fathom my feelings. It's Friday, Wilby having left on Wednesday, and I finish training and then pack in a blur. The dream is about to become real as we get ready to leave for Japan and our Britain team pre-Olympic holding camp.

The internet age, the dawning of Skype, has brought my world within easy reach. I call most of the guys back in Florida who I'll see in China. They're on my computer screen, sitting at home or wherever they happen to be getting ready for the same unknown. We're all a little apprehensive, not knowing what to expect of China, of the Games. Mostly, we avoid the theme of our fears and talk about nothing in particular.

Caroline Burckle delivers the exception: still over in America with the USA team, she has a drama to talk about and deal with. Jessica Hardy, America's No1 breaststroker, tested positive for a banned substance after making the team at the US Olympic trials. She gets dropped from the squad, her Beijing adventure over before it begins. The news breaks everywhere you look. Caroline says: "Jess is not the sort of person to take something, we are all speechless and confused."

They say of the Olympic Games that "anything can happen". Even so, events have taken an unexpected turn and I can't believe something as big as this can happen just two weeks before we get to Beijing.

I finish packing. Big-event nerves play a huge part in my preparation for the Games, my stay in Loughborough has much exceeded any expectations I had of it and will help me to cope with what is to come. I feel connected to a few individuals and ready to embark on my journey with the rest of the group, with far too much luggage that I haven't yet figured out how to carry!

Although I'm still very shy around a big group of people, unsure of myself around team members who all seem to know each other well and appear to be part of a tight clique, I embrace the situation for what it is, experience the discomfort and learn from it.

Dad meets me at Heathrow and takes some of my stuff. We say goodbye and he wishes me luck. Twelve hours later (I sleep most of the journey) and a short bus ride from the airport in Japan, we arrive at a 50-plus-storey hotel in Osaka. I'm sharing with Hannah Miley, the 400m medley swimmer. Our view is spectacular: miles of buildings interspersed with a spaghetti of roads hoisted high above the ground, providing shade for the life going on below it all. A small stretch of open water breaks up the mass of towering structures around us. From up here on high in our fantastic, temporary home, I can see for miles. I lose myself in the cityscape swirling below.

We take a two-stop ride on the train to the Osaka pool, the journey long enough for humidity to grip to the skin like an invisible leech. The alien chime announcing an incoming train resonates through the team as we alight; the sound will stay with us for the entire trip and beyond. So will the loud, obnoxious, vibration that accompanies us on the short walk to the pool. It turns out to be the noise of thousands of cricket-like bugs that live in the few trees and bushes along the way.

A short dip in the pool, a gentle, non-taxing swim, washes away the rust and dust of the journey and the day. My first swim has been a little over-whelming: a mass of new faces in the pool, and I'm still unsure of everyone's name. We take the two stops back to base, the station chime running back against the scale of the one we'd heard on arrival, allowing us to differentiate between the direction of incoming trains.

Back at the hotel, the media is waiting for us. My interview is scheduled to follow Jemma Lowe's. We sit in line in the hotel lobby for our turn in front of a camera or reporter's notebook. This tiny girl from Hartlepool is curled into the smallest space in a chair in front of me.

We had met before on a few British swimming camps but had always been a few friendships apart to make a connection. We knew of each other but didn't know each other. Her blonde hair and blue eyes strike me as we get to know each other and delve a little deeper into where we came from. The conversation turns to guys, a theme that always seems to take a chat between women into comfortable territory. Jemma discloses a few personal details of a previous relationship and I disclose a few tit-bits about "the Hobbit". We never get to my Mum, we never enter the world of pain or anxiety. There is safety at the surface.

It's the start of a glorious friendship between we two G/Jemmas. From here on, I'm more relaxed with my teammates and am better able to handle a whirlwind of new people and personalities, new friendships. Some treat me with kid gloves, someone to be handled with care, avoiding even the simplest of questions such as "are you Ok?" for fear of upsetting me. Others place no subject off limits, show no regard for my feelings, have no empathy with my situation. I simply have to deal with it, one way or another.

Whether they don't know about the death of my mother or whether they are unsure of me, or whether it is simply that they are so wrapped up in the rush of the Olympic Games thinking of themselves just as I am wrapped up in my own feelings, I cannot say.

I do know that I wish I could explain my feelings and talk about them. I wish I knew how to articulate my emotions: for my own sake, not for theirs. For now, however, there is nothing to say, the death of a parent swept beyond the conscious hours in which I'm embracing the here and now and the experience soon to come.

At dinner with a table of girls, I'm a couple of nights into this new start, in a new country, a new world. I laugh. I'm so at ease now that the nervous giggling and forced laughter that punctuated the start of this trip turns into genuine laughter, a place of warmth. It's been a good day: a good training set in the pool earlier and now real joy. For a fleeting moment, I wonder if all my anxiety and pent-up nervousness has been melted right here in this banter at dinner.

Socialising with my Britain teammates and discussing America really settles me. Between episodes of "Gossip Girl" on my laptop and playing on my new Nintendo DS, I feel as though I've entered a virtual realm a planet away from the reality of events in a world where a family loses a wife, a mother. My mother.

CHAPTER 14

The Olympic Games

"Have no fear of perfection- you'll never reach it."

— SALVADOR DALI

Beijing is another shock to the system. Only this time it's an overwhelmingly exciting shock. I feel like I've just won a million dollars, flown to the moon, danced with the stars and helped to eradicate world poverty, all on an endless supply of milk chocolate. My senses are on overdrive.

Our arrival in China is red-carpet: the country, sights, sounds, smells; the media on the march in pursuit of anything that moves; lights, videos, photographs of events at every turn. If I hadn't believed before this that I'd made the Olympics, I do now. On the coach journey from the airport, Mario Cart games on the DS are set aside in favour of soaking up spectacular views. A new world opens before our eyes. We get glimpses of what our Beijing abode will look like as our rite of Olympic passage rolls towards the village complete with police escort. I feel like some sort of celebrity!

Security at the entrance to the village is much like that at an airport, with a twist of local colour: an army of little Chinese volunteers, all dressed in blue, bustle about doing everything in their power to get us through the system quickly and without fuss. Past control, there are crowds of people, a legion of luggage in tow, and a feast of free food and drink. The swell of humanity around me sends my brain into overload. Stereotypes and pigeon holes are redundant in this melee of mankind.

I spot a group of Filipino swimmers. I know it's them because JB Walsh is standing there. He's a butterfly swimmer and fellow Gator at the University of Florida - and one of the most gentle, kind and sensitive guys I know. He's the boy I shared a room - platonically - with one night over the summer in Orlando when a group of non-American swimmers went on a weekend vacation to the water theme park Wet and Wild. I run over to him and give him a huge hug, both of us taking comfort in the familiarity of someone in a setting strikingly unfamiliar. The British team is staring at us as I talk and talk. They're wondering who this little Filipino guy is.

Excitement and happiness courses through my body, my mind reeling with the first impressions of a fantastic arrival in a spectacular place. The village is what it claims to be: houses, food places, gardens and even a red telephone box that looks as though it has just landed from London. In our apartment, we have red sofas, a TV, a fridge and there are two beds to every room, with drawings by Chinese children on the walls helping to make us feel at home the moment we walk through the door. Each six-person suite has three bedrooms: Caitlin McClatchey and I are in one room, Kate Haywood and Jo Jackson in another and Fran Halsall and Lizzie Simmonds in the other.

We take a shuttle bus to the pool. There's Caroline Burckle. I jump on her: I haven't seen her in a while and conversation rattles between us the entire 15-minute ride. A permanent smile plastered on my face, we share stories and imagine what the Water Cube pool is going to look like. We feel like we need pinching: are we really on this amazing journey together, truly blessed to be here?

I'm in my element as I get off the bus, take in the spectacular structure of the vast aquatics venue that does indeed look like a water cube, complete with what look like droplets covering the surface. The facility houses two 50-metre pools, in which I'm about to experience my first Olympic Games. I see most of my friends from Florida around the poolside and stop to catch up with each of them, the British team now my friends, the UF team my support system and family, all together under one roof, with coaches Anthony Nesty and Gregg Troy. I look up and whisper: "Mum, everything is going to be ok."

Back in the village, we scope out dinner. I'm dumbfounded by the magnitude of the canteen. A vast space filled with row-upon-row of tables and chairs surrounded by food stations, it looks like a school cafeteria on steroids. Each outlet serves food from a different country. In the far left-hand corner is McDonalds. Yes, that's right, some of the world's fittest athletes can eat as much as they want, for free, at any time of day and most of the night. So much excitement and chat, so many tales to tell, exchanges, sights and insights, sounds and smells in just the one day - yet I am still buzzing.

At dinner, I sit with Bradley and Omar from Florida and we meet another crowd from around the world, some friends of friends, some complete strangers. I'm on the edge of my chair, bursting with the thrill of it all, too hyper to sit still. At each food station there's a watermelon calved in the shape of Chinese symbols, the huge open room festooned in decoration and colour. Logos of Beijing 2008 are etched all over the walls, Coca Cola drink fridges line the walls, each one stocked with the real thing, plus Powerade, Sprite and milk. Help yourself.

We watch the opening ceremony on TV from the comfort of our room. Gator teammates Omar and Shaune, here for Colombia and the Cayman Islands respectively, relax with us in our patriotic British living room bedecked in red, white and blue. Swimming traditionally starts on the first day at the Olympics, putting the march into the stadium beyond the reach of almost all swimmers who come with medals in mind. The risk of exhaustion on the eve of having to be at our very best in the water is not worth taking.

The Chinese do not do things by half, not by any stretch of the imagination. The attention to detail in the captivating light show and fireworks fascinates me and has the rest of the world in awe. The flares and flashes of the fireworks are synchronized on our small screen and in the night sky of the real world just beyond our window. The double take is surreal.

It's better than any of the opening ceremonies that I had watched every four years sitting alongside Mum on the sofa back home. Tonight's spectacle not only brings me closer to her but reminds me that I'm taking this journey with her: no longer in our living room in England but here in China, first hand, the real deal. She is here in spirit, she is here in my head, my blood, my heart, my soul, experiencing everything with me.

If she were home now, watching this show from the same seat we always sat in; if she could see it all unfolding, she would be saying how fascinating it all is and commenting on the attention that's been paid to detail. She would also be watching with a sense of pride, excitement and anxiety. This opening ceremony would surely be different, if only because her little girl was part of it.

This one is different for me too. Watching the flag-bearers lead their country's athletes out with pride, I feel an overwhelming sense of joy. There's Bradley Ally, the boy who took me to dinner over the summer to help me to grieve, the boy who has his own troubles in life but still took the time to take me out, pay for me and listen to me. Bradley Ally is carrying the flag for Barbados: his smile is so wide that it looks like it might burst through his cheeks. The youthful beauty of his beaming face captures the thrill of it all. Mark Foster carries our flag with composure and pride, in keeping with his evident gratitude for having been granted this unique privilege.

Finally, Anthony Nesty, an Olympic champion in 1988, the first black swimmer ever to stand aloft a podium in the big race pool and now a coach in Florida, carries the flag for Surinam. He struts proudly with an air of grace and subdued happiness. His modesty, which graces my life every day back in Florida, shines through the potent concentration on his face, his gaze, focus and pride trained singularly on his duty and purpose.

Notes from my Olympic Diary:

August 10
Evening heats of the 100m backstroke: never been so nervous. Been thinking about it all day, butterflies in my stomach the whole time. It feels awful. 1min 00.11, sixth place among the 16 qualifiers.

That night: Tom Haffield comes in to our room to say 'hi', and so does Lizzie Simmonds. It's nice to know that we're still all relaxed in each other's company, to feel like I am really part of a team now, almost as close as Florida - it's wonderful!

August 11
Semi-final: nowhere near as nervous, I swim in the same heat as defending Olympic champion Natalie Coughlin, of the USA. I know I have to take the race out faster. A British record - 59.79, 5th fastest into the final - and I love it! It hurt a lot more than it had last night and I had diarrhoea REALLY badly all night and morning, and my neck was AWFUL where I'd slept funny - so hopefully there's room for improvement!

Missed Becky and Jo's swim: an amazing feat. First female gold in 48 years - and bronze in the same 400m freestyle race. Amazing. But I can't help but feel jealous. I feel a wave of envy: I wanted that so bad - it was my dream to end the drought. I even shared it with a couple of other swimmers and they said they had the exact same dream too, so luckily I wasn't the only person thinking it.

Stayed at the village, cleaned the room and watched the swimming on TV: a very chilled evening.

August 12

Not nervous at all before final, excited really. Like yesterday, I wake up and go to the pool a little earlier. Feeling very confident. Behind the blocks, I smile, and then as they call my name I see my Dad and bro on the big screen waving the British flag. I take the race out a little more controlled and come back as hard as I can. I look up at the scoreboard: 4th.

Natalie Coughlin has won in 58.96, 0.23sec ahead of Kirsty Coventry. The bronze has gone to Coughlin's teammate Margaret Hoelzer, in 59.34, just 0.04sec ahead of me.

Indescribable disappointment runs through my veins. I stare at the board for a while and just cannot find it in me to smile. I get through the interviews, tell the media that I'm disappointed but will be back four years from now.

I see [Anthony] Nesty on the way to the swim-down pool. Just seeing him makes me cry. I'm in tears until I see [Gregg] Troy - and then I cry a little more. Disappointment is not dulled by the British, European and Commonwealth records I just established. The intensity of disappointment is so deep that I have to force a smile each time someone says "well done". I cry some more. Fourth is just not what I came to China for.

At the team meeting, I stand to hear coach Ben Titley tell the team that if we step back and look at the real story, we will understand. He quotes something I said to Pat, the physiotherapist, when I was having my rub-down: "It just sucks when you know you were so close to gold". That, said Ben, said something positive about me not being here to win a medal but to win. Now I'm in the mood for a 200m, and then I'll look forward to the relay.

August 13

A day off: disappointment is still stewing in my bones. I watch the swimming on TV in the morning and then head to the pool at night. There's more disappointment around me - and along with that there is anger and frustration when the women's 4x200m freestyle relay team that could have - even would have - medalled doesn't even make the final because they rested two of the fastest swimmers in heats.

Caitlin even pulled out of the 100m solo to make it. Completely gutted, all round. Can't really put the blame on anyone ... but human nature steers us to blaming someone and that came down to Ben or the swimmers or Ben and the swimmers. Those close to Ben who know him better than I do blame him;

others who don't really know him don't know what to think. Gregor Tait and I share the same outlook: not really worth arguing over.

All of the British woes aside, there's good news from my Florida teammates: Brett swam a best time in his 200m back and Bradley made the semifinal in 5th for the 200 medley. So excited for him.

August 14

Get in and have a dip. Speak to Duncan [the psychologist] about how I am still really caught up on the 100. Through the conversation I realise that the loss of a gold was parallel to the loss of Mum. I try to pick myself up. Watched finals this morning until the breaststroke then came home to the village because I'm tired. Saw [Caroline] Burks on TV, and Ryan [Lochte]. Burks did amazing - a bronze medal in the 4x200m freestyle.

Tired, have a nap, then lunch. Watch a bit of a movie then go to the pool at night for 200m heats. Not really sure I want to swim at all, then get out there on the deck and smile and realise that I love swimming and that it is all about fun and the Games - so best give it a good shot. I swim just off my best and scrape through to the semis in 16th place. Lucky! I go home after seeing Dad and Peter, eat a big dinner and go to bed.

August 15

I feel Ok in the morning and come out of the race smiling and sporting a new personal best time, 2:09.19, half a second inside my previous fastest. It's the Olympic Games - and my best does not get me into the final: I miss the cut by 0.12sec. Frustrating. It's good to see Lizzie [Simmonds] go through to the final. I'll be there to cheer her on.

August 16

The show is coming to a close. Lizzie does a good job in the 200m backstroke final and we have the last pre-finals team meeting this evening. One more day to go.

August 17

The 4x100m medley relay. We have a great shot at the podium. When I get to the wall on backstroke I look up to great news: 59.05, a European record lead-off. Only the Olympic champion Natalie Coughlin goes faster, my time good enough to have won silver in the solo race days before. It wasn't to be but it's great to end on a high. The race unfolds, Australia, the USA and China the first three teams home as we scream for Fran to bring it home on freestyle. We take Russia - but it's that worst-of-all place for us again: 4th. It's agony. You'll often hear swimmers say how awful it is to finish 4th and how they'd rather be last than 4th. I know what they mean.

That night in the canteen, everyone is in a mood to let go. The job is done, the years of hard work behind us, the result in. Time to party. Nerves and passions are still on edge. The next days all blur into one. Meeting Jay - a pivotal moment in my life - initiation, pool and going out. China doll drinking and just letting our hair down after four years of discipline and routine.

CHAPTER 15

Jay

"Each relationship nurtures a strength or a weakness within you."

– MIKE MURDOCK

The comedown from a drug so severe that it leaves you numb is cruel. I fall with a thud. The Olympic high is followed by a low, the 'what next' an anticlimax that dominates all thought - and not only because the party is over.

Cold turkey of the emotional kind: adrenaline, excitement and true elation are among side effects, while meaningless, erotic encounters make the list too. But what happens when fanciful flirtation takes a hold and refuses to let go?

I meet Jay two days before flying home from Beijing, find out he is on the same flight back to the US and start texting him with the Chinese sim-card we got at one of the village shops. He texts back. He is keen, exciting and truly inspiring. He tells me things that sound incredible. They knock my experiences into a cocked hat, his life story makes mine sound like a breeze.

The things he has overcome on his way to being the person he is, on his way to the Olympic podium in a sport beyond mine, are . well, unbelievable. The boy and my fantasy of him have me on edge. I want, I need. On a high in another realm, using an alien phone number, I find myself transported from the harshness of the real world to another country, one in which a boy - I should say man - is making me feel as though I'm floating on a cloud of marsh-mallow and chocolate. My hormones are running wild.

The flight home is fun. We flirt, we talk a little and he tells me he writes a journal. He had already shown me some of his scribblings online but he had written his own personal journal since 1998. We have much in common - the overwhelming fire within me, a thirst for him intimidates me, floods my lungs as I try to make sense of this man.

I text him before we get on the plane: "Just fun; no emotions involved." It is my way of shielding my heart. The line is drawn, the rule laid down. Even so, the limited exchanges we've shared through messaging leave me wanting to know more about him. I need to understand Jay; not only because he's blazingly intelligent and strikingly handsome for an 'older' man, ten years my senior, but because I wonder whether knowing more about him might help me to understand more about myself.

"You intimidate me", I tell him. I explain that it is going to be hard for me to process any emotions now, given the weight of information he has shared with me and the things I have shared with him. The person he is, the things he has endured, the details of his own family bereavement, his role helping victims of the 9/11 attacks in New York: it has all come at me in a flood. He is a scary thought for me right now.I watch Jay dart up and down the huge 747 Boeing jet, charm his constant partner. He entrances and captivates almost every girl he walks past, every girl he introduces himself to. His obvious magnetism feeds my curiosity, though with each fleeting second of this slide into the unknown an alarm bell tolls through every bone in my body, warning me of the danger I'm sinking into. I ignore the threat, overwhelmed with a need for him.

Most of the plane is doing its best to snooze, lights out, a few watching a movie, their screens lending an eerie twilight to the cabin. I stand to stretch my legs and walk around the plane.

The small space between the bathrooms and the back seats of the plane shrinks in Jay's presence. We keep a respectable distance but the uncontrol-lable lust in me awakens like a sleeping monster. We're inches apart. It feels like miles. I melt at the beauty in his personality. The confidence in him awak-ens a flower in me. Utter desire takes over from lust.

I look deep into his enticing, gorgeous brown-green eyes. His "Hi" goes well beyond the standard greeting. Whether he intends it or not, there's a depth of meaning in his voice. It irritates me but I find myself drawn in.

"Every time you say 'Hi', you have to kiss me," I say, my heart skipping a beat, a steady voice masking my nervousness.

"Hmm . Hi," he replies, leaning in, closing the distance between us before kissing me so passionately that I lose myself for a brief few seconds and forget that I'm on a plane flying back to America. I embrace his passion, the romance taken for what I understand it to be. With warmth and a welcome touch, he holds me in his arms. I feel complete, if only for a moment. Fireworks explode in my heart. I feel safe.

Jay is a womaniser. I tell him so and he's offended - but he is. He seems to know almost everyone on the plane; he flirts with almost every girl he lays his eyes on. Yet still I'm drawn in, I want to know more. No emotions, just fun, I remind myself.

My brain tells me that this is not a good idea, that I'll get hurt, that I will not see him again after this flight, that it would be impossible to have a relationship with this charming, flirtatious Casanova. Then there's his age. He's about 10 years older than me. And yet, my heart talks back ... maybe he's a chance worth taking. I want more.

I come to an understanding with my own feelings: the flirtation was fun; I loved it; I just wish my emotions were not quite so intense. It leaves me with an all-too-familiar sense of loss.

Trying to deal with the comedown from what happened and what might have been is not my idea of fun. Trying to explain my feelings to people is almost impossible. Intrusive thoughts enter my mind 'Unless you were there, you wouldn't get it, wouldn't know how I felt.' It leaves me in a lonely place. Depression creeps through me, unruly and inexplicable.

I manage to mention it to Caroline but the best remedy, I find, is jet lag: tiredness, a touch of mental fatigue in the mix, sends me into a deep slumber, a place of safety from the need to socialise, the need to think. On the one hand, I want very much to socialise and get back to normal but on the other hand I need to escape. I want to return to my "holiday from reality": the real stuff is depressing, boring and de-motivating, I think to myself.

It is just a way of avoiding the issue, like water flowing round a rock in its path. When you can't even understand your own emotions, how are you supposed to explain them to someone else?

The empty shell in which I've been able to hide gradually peels away during the first week back home from Beijing as reality returns with an avalanche of escalating emotions. This reality feels unreal. I feel as though I simply exist while the world I can't connect with spins around me.

CHAPTER

16

Meeting the Queen

"The important thing is not what they think of me, but of what I think of them"

— QUEEN VICTORIA

A whirlwind, a dream, it all feels so unreal. Nothing about this week seems normal. I'm flying home to Britain and I feel euphoric: I'm not travelling home to illness, to family sadness, not even for a holiday. This time, I'm off to meet the Queen.

The British Olympic team gathers at Guildhall in the City, the square mile in the heart of London. We're in a sea of people, all sorts of VIPs, officials and politicians. They're on the move, seeing if there's someone more important to speak to along the line. They seem to be almost as excited (if not more so) than the rest of us. The sight of Britain doing what it has long been Olympic champion at, pomp and ceremony, is quite something.

The guards at Buckingham Palace mingle in the crowd and let the medallists from the team don their busbies, those tall furry hats that have become a hallmark of London, in exchange for a souvenir snap to take home to the family and one day show the grandkids.

There's a buzz in the air, quite literally, the team murmur incessant as we assemble in readiness to board the flat-bed lorries that will sweep us through streets of London apparently lined with well-wishers who've come out to congratulate the best result at a Games Britain has ever had.

I'm not sure what to expect: is anyone really going to stand there in the cold of a mid-October lunchtime to cheer for a load of athletes who did something in China a couple of months back? Well, the answer is a resounding 'yes'.

As we make our way through the capital, thousands of people surround the floats, cheering, running alongside and waving giant blue-foam fingers in the shape of the National Lottery logo. We arrive in Trafalgar Square to a hero's welcome.

They've built a temporary stage that seems to fill the square. We leave the floats and sit down in seats facing the crowd before listening to London's Mayor, Boris Johnson, deliver a rather entertaining speech that shows he's looking forward to the London 2012 Games like much of the rest of the country.

We're all in our Olympic track suits. It's chilly and some of the people leaning over the barriers have mugs of steaming hot chocolate in their hands. I wish I could lean over and grab one. There's something surreal about sitting here in this historic square surrounded by monuments that speak of the stuff our land is made of. I take in the faces in the crowd, picking out the odd one to study. It's like a painting, a snap shot in time but one that includes me. I'm looking at it from within.

These people are so thrilled to see us, pride and joy etched on their faces as they wave at us. I've never truly felt that connection to my country before, neither for England nor Britain, beyond the pride we all take in wearing national colours when we compete. Here, in this much wider setting, I'm able to be a part of that patriotism, able to be and feel British.

It helps to sit in such a grandiose place. London is like that: you're engulfed in history, you feel the weight of generations, the passing of time, the creation of a land and its people. It is humbling, overwhelming, stirring and somehow comforting all at once. It is definitely not like America, where many of the towns and cities you visit were born during Queen Victoria's early reign.

The parade ends. We make our way back to the hotel, have some food and relax for a couple of hours before it's time to get changed for the reception tonight. We climb back on the buses. Dusk descends, the twilight dotted by the twinkle of street lamps, London in the first throes of autumn, thoughts already turning to Christmas, time racing on.

Up ahead, the majestic, golden gates of the Palace come into view. I recall them as having always been permanently closed. Today, they are open - for us. It's the stuff of fairytales: we walk along a red carpet, ascend a staircase of gold and white. I'm slightly dazed. It's unbelievable. Upstairs, we mingle with members of the Royal household: the Anne, the Princess Royal and Camilla, Duchess of Cornwall, are smiling, chatting and shaking hands.

This is the first time that the team has been together and enjoying each other's company since Beijing. We're all dressed in our formal Games outfits so there's no sense of anyone standing out or making a show. The catering staff stand out more as they float through the room in their uniforms tempting us with nibbles and glasses of champagne or orange juice and water. I'm too excited to be hungry. Besides, we have a team dinner back at the hotel. When I take a glass, I stick to the non-alcoholic options, conscious of not making a spectacle of myself!

Queen Elizabeth II greets the medallists first and then comes through to meet us in this vast, open, tall auditorium with chandeliers hanging from the ceilings, the walls and drapes, furniture and fittings as royal as you would expect them to be. There's a lot of red and gold; very palatial.

Up at my height, Her Majesty is so short in her blue dress. When she's introduced to us, we can't help but notice the very proper accent she speaks in. I suppose that's why they call it "the Queen's English". Here we are, me, Kate Haywood and Ellen Gandy, meeting the Queen. It feels like we're on some movie set.

The monarch is very together, very with it. It is obvious that she does this kind of stuff all the time. She's very professional, her pleasantness and professionalism to the fore as she works her way across the room.

Suddenly, she is right here in front of us. We're all very nervous and it shows. The Queen asks us something about the Games and we all say something in reply. Precisely what was said, I will never quite remember. As soon as she moved on, I looked at the other two: we were all in a state of slight shock and awe. "What did I say?" I ask Kate and Ellen. They shrugged and laughed. Kate said it was "really cool" to meet the Queen and Ellen was excited too. My mind had gone blank. I know I said something and I'm left wondering not only whether it was a load of incomprehensible nonsense but whether I'd come across as an American because of the accent that has all but drowned out the southern English lilt I once had.

After the reception, we're free to go off and spend time with friends. A group of us head to Mahiki, a cocktail bar in Dover Street. The theme is tropical and there's a treasure chest loaded with alcohol. I've no idea who a lot of the other Olympic athletes are, even before I drink far too much. There's a jockey at the bar and we end up dancing a lot. He's a cool guy but he's about half my height! I drift off and then fall asleep on Dave Davies' shoulder. He can take it, what with all that training for the 1500m (he got bronze in Athens back in 2004) and the marathon (and silver in Beijing).

The last thing my Dad had told me before the reception, knowing I would go out partying, was "figure out how you're going to get back to your hotel ... it's London". The best I'd done was to put a small map book in my pocket but that was useless because I was too drunk to see the page properly. Everything was a blur and I felt really sick.

Under the circumstances, I did amazingly well: I eventually made it back to my hotel, though quite how I did it remains a mystery. Along the way, I had one self-imagined crisis as I walked past a hotel that I thought might be mine before realising that it wasn't: the porter came forward and asked if I'd like him to get me a cab but I just thought he was a bad guy and shouted at him to get away from me.

A couple of days later, I'm on the plane back to America and a very different world.

Christmas In New York

"Your task is not to seek for love but merely to seek and find all the barriers within yourself that you have built against it."

— RUMI

Christmas 2008, the first festive season since Mum died. Dad and my brother Peter have joined me in New York. We're doing the whole tourist thing, taking in the iconic sights, the giant tree in Times Square: anything to avoid being where we'd been and doing what we'd done when Mum was there, all those things that would have frozen us in a time and place that will now only ever be a memory.We're constantly on the go, biting into bits of the Big Apple, keeping busy, having fun, celebrating the American way. It was a deliberate decision, one we all agreed on - and it's working. What an amazing Christmas.

We wake up on the morning of the 25th at Liz Goldson's Dad's house, open presents and delve into stockings. It makes for a great start to this festive day before we travel over to Liz's Mom's house for lunch. From the moment we walk in, their rescue dog Mya takes a dislike to Dad. I think it's a size thing: Dad's big and the usually-larger-than-life, black mutt is terrified. I feel so sorry for my old man: he's trying so hard to be gentle and have the dog take to him but his efforts are all in vain. Mya's having none of it.

As for the rest of the Goldson family ... they're just so beautiful. The children are of mixed race and Liz's younger brother was at the front of the queue when looks and personality were given out: a model, he's stunning, very skinny and really fun to be around.

Liz has been a wonderful friend of mine since the moment she moved in with me back in Gainesville. We've been through a lot together, including a really scary moment when she had too much to drink in a club and found herself surrounded by football players. I'm aware of that scene: I have a deep dislike and distrust of it and avoid it. I could see all the warning signs. I dragged Liz out of the club; she slapped me. She had no recollection of that the next day.

She did thank me, though, for getting her out of what she knew could have been a dangerous situation. Liz is very much aware of things that are not quite what they seem to be. Take her culinary skills: she's an amazing cook, she can turn anything into a feast. It also became apparent that while she could cook anything, she could not always eat it herself. At first she dealt with bulimia on her own, enduring the symptoms of a horrendous illness in silence. Only later did she find the strength to start a healing process in learning how to get through it, via rehabilitation in Philadelphia.

She slipped into bulimia in the way that many do: by looking in the mirror and seeing something that she perceived to be less than perfect. It's never quite as simple as that, of course, and back in Florida it took a long time and a lot of trust for her to confide in me and those around her. She swam for the Gators before her illness overtook her body and prevented her from continuing with the sport. She came to watch the South-Eastern Conference Championships with my Dad who recognised a few tell-tale signs.

Her weakness, if you can call it that, stems from her strength: Liz is someone who, no matter what it is she's dealing with, will accept nothing less than giving it her all, doing things to the best of her ability and then taking a view as to whether she's matched up to the standard she sets for herself. In the pool and at school she worked really hard, always striving to be the very best she could be. It was the same when she got a job as a bartender in Gainesville: she didn't just serve drinks, she took it upon herself to study the whole thing, to know how to mix even the drinks no-one was ever going to buy. Everything was above and beyond the call. The motivation and dedication she portrays inspires me immensely.

She's incredibly competitive, no matter what she's doing: cooking, baking, even cleaning. When she lived with us, the house was always spotless, there was always food being cooked and if we had a party the place would be festooned with decorations every way you looked. She's outgoing and lights up a room the moment she steps through the door.

That love for life made me want to be around her all the time and here she is now bringing all of those wonderful qualities to the Christmas table on this magical day, her whole family here, me, my Dad and my brother feeling most privileged. It is great fun, we have a wonderful time, one that stands in stark contrast to last Christmas, when we were barely understanding our lives.

I remember that we put up the decorations back home, tried to do the usual things - but it was just not Christmas. Our rock was crumbling and we had no appetite to be merry, good tidings a remote hope.

Little wonder that it feels so much better this year to find ourselves in a very different place. To be away, just the three of us with Liz's family, feels as though there's been a great release from the weight of sadness we've all endured. It isn't that Mum is not in our thoughts (in fact, she's all but constantly in them) but we're having so much fun and the many distractions make it easier not to think about her all the time.

There's something else on my mind too. Jay is in New Jersey and he's coming to town to see me. He's booked a table at the New York Athletic Club overlooking Central Park. I'm thrilled to see him again. Through my eyes, here is a potential partner for me, a man on a pedestal, someone who has everything that I would want; someone I could potentially see myself with for a number of years. His skills and brain are beyond mine and he is leading the kind of life that I do not but would like to.

The traits of a womaniser are all over him. I'm aware of that: the way he talks to me is just too smooth for it not to be an act. He does it to others too. Yet right here in this amazing place at a time when my emotions are raw, he still makes me giddy and leaves me longing to know - and want - more.

Later, I will feel differently, later I will find time to reconcile my contradictory feelings, later I will find it hard to overcome this trail of emotion. Today, Jay is where I think I want to be. Although he is 10 years older than me, he seems to be on my level when it comes to interests and someone whose experience in life exceeds mine and will help me to grow.

What he feels as we sit here, I'm not sure. He probably sees a potential one-night stand. I see everything as an advance and everything he's saying as an indication that he is genuinely interested in me and wants to get to know me as a person. He has engaged in phone calls, text messages and emails in the manner of someone who certainly wanted my friendship. I see him as interested enough to take the next step.

We enjoy an amazing dinner, some fantastic company and conversation that brings back to mind lots of things that I'd stored away in memory for a while. By the time the evening draws to a close, I feel I've been on a fine date in a picturesque setting. There's a touch of fairytale about it. By the time I get back to Liz's house, I'm still giddy with the thrill of it all. I'm met by a different mood. Liz doesn't like Jay because of the way he's been with me and the way I've been with him - as she sees it.

My Dad has met him today and didn't really like him either. They didn't gel. Jay's a talker. He will talk about a lot of things all at the same time, flitting from one thought and subject to another. Sometimes he says what needs to be said but he'll talk it to death and some more until you simply don't care what he's saying anymore.

Often, our exchanges have been very one-sided. He sets the pace and decides when to engage and when not. However, I still spend my time pining and wanting to talk to him. It can be immensely irritating. He will text me a 'hi', I respond but then there's no reply. I think, "look, if you're not going to engage in conversation, don't start a conversation".

It's for that very reason that none of my friends like him. Peter, my brother, has a different reason. He's super intelligent. Jay's highly clever too. I don't know my facts to quite the same intense degree as they do. Where I listen to Jay to hear what he has to say and learn something I might not have known, Peter listens to him at the same pitch - and shows he is willing to go into battle if there something he deems wrong or misinformed.

My brother can be confrontational. He's almost like a lawyer in the way he argues: he has a way of dealing with people and getting out of them what he needs; gaining an understanding about what they're really about.

Against that backdrop, it's apparent here in New York this Christmas that I'm not going to gel with Jay on an emotional level: neither my Dad nor my brother nor my friends like him. And yet I'm still drawn: I want to know more about him and want him in my life.

I see a lot of good things in him, I'm impressed by the amazing things he's done in his life and his ever-positive personality always makes me smile. I feel as though he somehow fills a void that Mum's passing has left. I am, right now, lonely. I have great friends, like Liz, and a great family too, but the physical distance between England and Florida and the way we've been communicating has left me wishing we could be closer than we've been of late.

The truth is that I'm filling emotional gaps with Jay, with keeping busy, with whatever and whoever else happens to be there at any given moment.

It leaves me in turmoil. There have been times when I haven't spoken to him and times when I've tried to rid him from my life because I've seen him as a talker, all words but no action. Then I have had second thoughts: when it comes down to it he's done so much to help me in life and I gain so much from talking to him.

Conflict rages within me: I want more but what I'm really doing is trying to fill the void left by Mum with someone who could never match up to that, never fill that unique role. I love my Dad and my brother very much but, even there, there is not quite the same connection that I have with Mum, had with Mum. I can talk to Jay about things that I would not talk about with Dad and Peter and in that sense I see Jay filling the gap left by Mum all the more keenly.

Not that my openness is reciprocated: I tell Jay a lot about myself but he never gives anything up. If we go down that track of me asking the questions, he changes the subject and brings it straight back to me. He will inspire me to become a crisis counsellor within a year of our Christmas in the Big Apple - and I'll come to recognise the technique he uses. Here and now, it leaves me both frustrated because I can't get out of him what I want to know, and relieved as well, because I can finally talk about me and focus on my issues.

The theme of filling the void left by Mum will play out in every relationship I have in this period of my life. The truth is that we learn through experience but some experience is more permanent. When Mum was here, she would check up on me, call to see how I'm doing and I sometimes got sick of it and I'd say, "stop calling all the time!" When the calls ended with her life, I felt like I was missing a limb. Maybe I always will.

What's missing from any friendships and relationships I've had is the unconditional love, the stuff that comes with parenthood for some people: it doesn't matter what you do, how much you screw up, how much you change, they are there. If you need them, they are always there. You can cross a line with friends and they just don't come back. Parents do. For me, they were always there no matter what. Mum can be there no longer, not on a phone call, not in an email, not in person, not for a hug.

After the Christmas break, Dad and Peter head home to England and I head home to Florida to end-of-year training before partying my way into 2009. I stick to a promise I've made to myself as I bring in the New Year: I go out, party long and hard and have great fun.

Jay is back in New Jersey. I'm glad. I think that's been part of the attraction of the people I've picked as potential partners so far: there's a connection but I don't want them there all the time. I've never wanted to live in someone's pocket. I return to training with a spring in my step and feeling motivated by a festive season that has given us all so much to be thankful for. I need the independence that distance has granted me in all my relationships.

Just as well. By the time I swim at my second Olympics, I will not have met Jay in person again for almost four years. He promises to visit but never does. Skyping will be the closest we ever get to each other.

Two years on from our Christmas in New York, my take on events will be altered: I will be able to listen to him talk, maybe once a month, smile at the calm and collected man on the screen but know that there's nothing more than fun and friendship there. The pull I once felt is gone for good.

CHAPTER 18

Success, Summer and Felipe

"We become aware of the void as we fill it."

– ANTONIO PORCHIA

After the New Year partying is done, I pick up where I'd left off before Christmas and commit to some serious discipline, dedication and hard work. It's where I want to be. It's where I need to be. I'm not only focusing on me but taking a tip from Jay and looking to help others as a way of nurturing myself.

This 2008-2009 college swim season, I step up to honorary captain of the Gator women's team, helping the two others girls older than me who are actual team captains: the coaches feel that the team could do with input from someone who has competed at international level. People come to me and seem to enjoy my leadership but I'm working with two teammates and we all have a different approach.

It works well. The South Eastern Conference (SEC) title meet is being held in late February this year in Auburn, Alabama. I win all three of my events, the 100 and 200 yards backstroke for the second consecutive year, and set a National Collegiate Athletic Association record in the 200 yards backstroke (1min 48.34sec). Yards is no longer swum anywhere else in the world. The distances leave you shy of what you would cover in an international-standard metres pool and the difference in times on the clock make it hard for anyone outside to figure out how well we're going on the way to international duty in the summer ahead.

The team is going well and having a lot of fun as we bawl and cheer our way through every race, each session a nail-biter on the leaderboard. It comes down to the last relay: sprint freestyle and I'm last to go. My takeover is insane, better than anyone else's but more troublesome too. I take two jumps on the blocks: I start at the back of block, wind forward, jump to the edge of the block and then go.

The timing shows my reaction off the block as the moment my jump impacted on the block. I look up: victory! Followed by disqualified. That leaves us in second overall. All the coaches know straightaway what had happened and I am furious. There's nothing in the rules on relay starts that says that a swimmer can't jump on the blocks before leaping into the water. The toes leaving the block register the start, so any hop towards the moment you actually do leave the block to dive should not register as the start of a dive.

The coaches lodge a protest and the judges watch the video playback. Everyone waits nervously. It was obvious on the video that I hadn't left the blocks before my teammate's hand hits the wall. My reaction time is also slower than those registered in the lanes next to me. The momentum I gained with the jump forward produced momentum for a better dive than my rivals had but there was no way I false-started.

The judges accept that and, after some heart-stopping moments, we're reinstated, win the relay and take the overall SEC title back from Auburn, 744 points to the 730.5 score for the meet hosts. It's been the third-closest competition in SEC history, Georgia third, with 725. It's the first time since 2002 that the Gators girls get to take the trophy home to Gainesville to make it 17 victories in all since 1982.

Wilby, once more, was the hero who worked it all out and came to my rescue. He lodged the protest and got them to watch the video. It says a lot for the American way of doing things. If it had been an international meet, we would have stayed disqualified because the international swimming federation, FINA, does not allow video evidence to be used in appeals against disqualification. There's been a big debate about it but a vote on introducing video evidence will not be taken until 2013 at the earliest. That'll be more than 10 years after coaches and teams called for change.

Instant justice was what Wilby and the Gators were after - and the system delivered. When we talk about "family" in sport, that's what it comes down to: full backing in all eventualities. That's when you feel that family connection. It is never just about swimming but much more. Take the first words spoken by head coach Gregg Troy after we'd won the meet: "I am so proud of both our men (second overall) and women's teams. They really brought it tonight. Gemma Spofforth has been outstanding, not only in the pool, but as a leader of this team."

That, more than my wins, the record and the accolade of being named SEC Female Swimmer of the Year, made me really proud of what I'd achieved. it's not about me but the improvements my teammates and surrogate family have made together over the year.

There was more celebrating a few weeks later when we close the 2009 NCAA Championship meet with our 100th national event title, two school records and a seventh-place finish overall at College Station, Brazos County, Texas. On the last day of the meet, I win that 100th crown in the 200 yards backstroke, with teammates Teresa Crippen and Stephanie Proud making it a podium wipeout for the Gators at the Student Recreational Center Natatorium. The three of us are now the fastest three all-time from the University of Florida over 200 yards. It reflects the kind of competition we give each other daily in training.

Our men finished second at SECs. It was a great year for the Gators, coaches and swimmers. I get nominated for the Swimming and Diving Honda Sports Award as best SEC women swimmer of the season; the winner of that is named as a candidate for the Honda-Broderick Cup, awarded annually to the Collegiate Woman of the Year.

On the short list with me are Julia Smit (Stanford University), Olympic 200m breaststroke champion Rebecca Soni (University of Southern California) and a swimmer on her way to becoming an Olympic champion, Dana Vollmer (University of California, Berkeley). As the 2009 college season nears a close, one of the most formative years of my life, I am blessed by being awarded the University of Florida's Ben Hill-Griffin award for volunteering, academics and sports.

The focus now shifts to the World Championships, to be staged in Rome in July. I opt to miss British trials this spring and aim for a time good enough to qualify at the Scottish National Championships in June. That leaves me time to make the transition from the college season to the summer long-course season in 50m pools.

One of the test events at a time of hard training is the Charlotte Ultraswim, part of the USA Swimming Grand Prix circuit. As usual mid-season, my times are far from where I'll be when I've rested to race from peak - and there's something far more significant about the meet this year: it's where my next candid affair begins.

Without warning, I suddenly find myself drawn uncontrollably into having a physical relationship with an exotic young man I'd developed a crush on over the past couple of months. His deep, dark, beautiful eyes hooked me from the moment we had our first, clumsy encounter.

My affair with Felipe came down to the pure physical need of two consenting adults and nothing more. There was no emotional level to it beyond a profound animalistic instinct. The simple act of intercourse is almost at the other end of the scale of emotions to the bond between a mother and a daughter and yet, somehow I felt that satisfying my physical need was also helping me to heal on another level. I felt like the sex was yellow, the hole in my heart blue. Through experience, I would come to realise that that is not how it works and my yellow and blue produced a rather sickly looking green.

He is standing quietly, as he always does, waiting to leave the morning heats when I approach him and ask innocently: "What are you doing for lunch?"

Without hesitation, he replies: "I'm doing you for lunch."

"Ok!"

"No I'm doing YOU for lunch," he says, as if I hadn't understood what he was saying. His eyes entrance me. He's gorgeous. I smile, say "Ok" but think no more of it. Later that day as I relax in my hotel room between sessions I get a text: "So what to me doing you for lunch then?"

So, he really means it? I'm a little taken aback but play along. It might be fun. Certainly a great distraction from anything else I might be thinking about, so why not. Act follows self-justification. Back at the pool in the afternoon, we swim and chat as though nothing has happened, our secret rendezvous on the 15th floor of our hotel, the surreptitious connection known only to us satisfying the "yellow" need for sex and the "blue void" in me.

It sounds bizarre to link sexual desire and act with someone I barely know with the loss of my mother and the hurt that lives in me constantly but in my current emotional state, it makes sense to me. Grief has a strong grip on me. It turns in my brain like an old-fashioned towel wringer, twisting the towel so tight that the gushing can't stop until every droplet has been squeezed out.

In truth, I'm sick with anxiety: will I never be able to allow myself to connect emotionally to a man because of the pain and fear of losing someone close to me? Later, I will be sickened too by the notion that sex could possibly balance out the emptiness left behind by the loss of Mum, her whirlwind personality and all that she blew into my life to make me who I am.

Yet, right here today in Charlotte, it is all justified and balanced for a moment in my heart and mind. My exotic new play toy was available whenever I wanted him. Never emotionally available, but that wasn't what it was all about. I craved him physically. Continuing the affair might have been the mistake of the year. Fate lent a timely hand: Felipe was out of town for several weeks. I handle it well until another friend, his brother, Roberto, asks me if I miss my playmate. Actually, no, is my reply. In fact, I don't miss him at all. Sure, I miss having someone come over to the house; I miss being able to text him whenever I need connection. I don't miss him at all.

I start to think all too deeply about what it all means and find myself sliding back into depression. I come to the view that the "yellow" and "blue" are not in any way correlated. The connection I made was a false one, a fake.

Through a maze of thought, I conclude that the affair has to stop. I don't need any casual, unnerving affiliation. I don't need him; I don't need or particularly like what he can offer.

It is dawning on me: I have been trying to bury my complex emotional deprivation in the dolorous act of sex with each of the boys I have slept with in the past year. There have been a few encounters. It is unconventional and illogical. I've been equating things that do not equate. To put it simply, I've been using sex to bypass my inability to connect emotionally because of the death of my mother.

There is relief in realisation but the road ahead is far from clear. All I know is that I must point myself and my energies in a wholly different direction.

The water is my salvation.

The clock ticks, time to travel to Scotland for the national championships. Despite all the turmoil, the one thing that has been consistent has been my dedication to swimming, to discipline and hard work. In 59.56sec over 100m backstroke, I qualify for the world championships. In the 200m, I crack the British record and leave it at 2min 07.56sec, my times in line with the stake I'd claimed earlier in the year in college competition.

I feel buoyed. It has all been worth it. I am on my way to Rome and the 2009 world championships.

Chapter 19

Ready In Rome

"Reach for the moon, because even if you miss, you will land among the stars"

– UNKNOWN

Elation and a happy mood engulf me in Italy at the 2009 World Championships. All week long there are few moments when I feel tired, or even need to sleep. I am on a high all the time. It's been that way in the pool for much of the season and by the time departure day arrives, I am feeling great. Energy runs through me and around me. I am already on top of the world and the feeling simply grows stronger with each passing day.The Eternal City. It is electrifying to be here.

Rome is full of shadows, metaphoric and real. History at every corner, every turn of the head. The buildings, the structures, the living canvas of sharply contrasting yellow light and deep shadow that sweeps and transforms the city, gives me a sense of the spiritual, the beautiful, the spectacular. I feel welcome, there is a warmth here, I feel the presence of the people of this place and the monumental events that unfolded here.

If the city is eternal so it seems is the sunshine that bathes the man-made in natural glory and lifts the spirit. The stage is set for success in the pool too.

We are outdoors in the Foro Italico and by the time evening semi-finals and finals come round. The Foro is like a theatre of dreams, half in shade, half in light, the contrast sharp; thumbs up, thumbs down, the mood crisp, the air charged. I love being outdoors, in nature: this is not just a pool with a lane you have to swim in but an arena, the crowd connected, the rays of intense evening light reflected in the sparkle of water alive with its own energy. It's big for me.

I feel really fit, fitter, in fact, than ever before and my confidence and expectation are finely balanced. I know what I have to do and know I'm capable of doing it. Excitement mounts. I am ready to embrace and revel in this experience.

There are many factors to performance on any given day of a given year at a specific place in time. Who you room with can make a big difference. Here in Rome, I'm sharing with Jemma Lowe. The same tiny, blonde girl from last year's Olympics, now living out in Florida with me.

We've developed a great friendship. I love her for her honesty and her loyalty. She will tell you what she thinks and stick by you 100 per cent if you're her friend, and if you're not, her opinion will not waiver. That's made some people wary of her but once you get past the wall she seems to put up, the friendship waiting to be forged is the best, the struggle more than worth it.

She once admitted to me that when she was younger and a member of the Smart Track programme put together in Britain by Australian coach Bill Sweetenham, she thought I was weird, 'that strange girl that nobody liked, the one who didn't fit'. We figured out there was more to both of us than meets the eye.

During the championships, she's a great help to me. She's a great listener and she knows how to have fun. When I'm not skyping with friends back in Florida and with Jay, still in contact almost every day, I'm sitting on the bed with Jemma, the two of us screwing up our faces and grunging at the mac photo booth before falling about laughing. We don't talk swimming much, the topics of conversation miles from the pool: boys, books, the city, hopes and dryland dreams.

And chocolate. We're both chocoholics. I quit chocolate six weeks before the championships in a bet with coach Wilby. His part of the bargain: no more chewing tobacco. I managed the six weeks, my willpower fed by his commitment and the belief that the loss of something I really craved would be good for me. We endured because we were adamant that neither of us would let the other down. Wilby hasn't chewed again to this day and probably never will. His wife, Jill, is very happy with me!

Not that any of that will keep me from chocolate in the future. In fact, here I stand with Jemma in a shop in Rome lined with bars and boxes of chocolates. We fill our bags with the stuff and squirrel it back to our room. The fridge is full of forbidden fruit. Every day we open the door, stare longingly at the chocolate, look at each other and say "Ok, let's just have one now." Then we rethink: no, no, no. we've come so far!

There's a job to be done, a whole load of hard work and the dedication of a team of people to be respected. As I lay on the massage bench chatting to Pat Dunleavy, the physiotherapist I've known since my days as a junior at Portsmouth Northsea, I'm reminded of a book I once read in which it was said that it takes 10,000 hours to excel at anything.

I've done more than 10,000 hours of swimming but these past five or six weeks of pure discipline in my diet, pure discipline in training have made a truly significant difference.

I've been so determined. At the pool, I've been doing whatever it took. Outside the pool, I've been filling every waking moment. Even at night I've been away from home, sleeping in the dorms with the kids at summer camp for several weeks leading up to my final preparations for Rome. My days have been non-stop: at camp, I taught the kids to swim, then went to class at college and either side of all of that I trained with the squad morning and evening. At practice, I felt as though I had to leave it all in the pool and move on ready to go to the next thing.

The distractions of everything that followed training somehow allowed me to be very focused in the pool and kept me on the perfect diet: I was off chocolate, eating the right food and with no time to snack in between. I lost a lot of weight, though the correlation between swimming fast and weight is not a simple one.

I rarely get on the scales, the number staring back likely to reflect the amount of water weight in me at any given moment. I may be heavier on the scales but actually feel better in the water and swimming faster. I've learnt to go on what I feel, in the water, in my clothes, and not what the scales say.

Swimming teaches you how to listen to your body. Heartening is the moment when the right feel is backed up by the right numbers on the clock.

The runes read well before Rome. We have a test set in training that starts out as 10 times 100m, starting each of the 100m every 6 minutes. The swim takes about a minute flat out. The rest period of about 5 minutes has to be big enough for each of the ten 100m swims to be flat out. The next time we do the set, we do just eight 100m; then six times 100m, then four, then finally, close to the big meet, two 100m speed tests. By then, you're looking to get as close to race pace as possible. There's pride at stake because you're racing alongside everyone else in the squad.

Before Rome, each set was pretty good and I was proud of that. The moment came for the last two 100m tests in training. "Wow!" is all I can say after the last one: 1min 01sec. I'd never done anything like that in training. I'm a very different swimmer when it comes to putting a race suit on come the big day. I get a lot faster as we go through taper, the time when we start to ease back on the hard work so that we're sharp, ready to race in peak form. Come the big meet, the race suit replaces the baggier training suits we wear day to day and I know I will swim fast.

Coach Troy is big on that: we never train in our best suits. The race suits suck your bum in, make you feel smooth on top of the water. You feel good - an uplifting sensation that would be diminished if you got used to it by wearing a race suit every day in practice.

In Rome, the suits are a big issue. The suit makers have tents lined up in the tunnels between the warm-down pool and the main competition pool where swimmers can pick up a bodysuit for use in one race to avoid them being disadvantaged. We've never known this before in the sport. A lot of people are worried about what to wear, whether their suit will pop or rip. There is a lot of confusion around the whole issue. Suits are ripping and splitting on people. Some people will get through 10 suits (at more than $700 each) this week. Its a new suit per race for many. Thankfully, the suitmakers had been obliged to make sure their products are available free of charge in the interests of as level a playing field as possible, if possible under such circumstances.

In 2008, Speedo made the LZR racer, a suit half made up of polyurethane panels, the first time race apparel had been made of non-textile materials. Everyone's times are faster, some gains far greater than others.

Leading into Rome, I've tried lots of different suits, including the new full body 100% polyurethane, neoprene or other non-textile apparel that most swimmers are wearing. They have twice as much non-textile material in them as the LZR does but they just don't sit well for me. I don't feel fast, I don't feel like they are generating speed for me. Everyone is saying they feel so fast in what Craig Lord, of The Times, dubbed "the shiny suits" because when wet you can see your reflection in the surface of something that looks like tight rubber.

The morning of the 100m backstroke heats arrives and I'm sticking to my LZR. I have a different worry: I've brought the wrong cap and goggles to the ready room where we all gather before races. Wilby rushes off to scrounge a cap and goggles from someone. I'm calm. I feel fine and it shows: in the 11th of 12 heats, I go 58.78sec, a World-Championship meet record, the first sub-59sec in the history of the global event and inside the European record of 59.05 I set leading Britain's Olympic medley relay off in Beijing last year.

I'm just 0.01sec shy of the world record held by Kirsty Coventry, a Zimbabwean who, like me, is based in the US. I look up at the board and think I see a 59-plus but there's a No 1 after my name. How can I be first when Australian Emily Seebohm has gone a 59.64 and me a .78? I then realise I've gone 58-plus. Big smile. Amazing. I felt good in the water, really strong, stronger than I imagined I would feel.

Kirsty is up next in the last heat of the morning and swims 59.51. The closest to me is Anastasia Zueva, of Russia, on 59.01. The potential for a great result in the final tomorrow is very real.

The pressure for me to wear a 2009-model suit, the full non-textile number, comes from all sides: Michael Scott, the Britain performance director, Dennis Pursley, the head coach, even Wilby, just about everyone pulls me aside and says 'you need to wear the suit'. I get the message: they wouldn't be happy if I didn't. But I can't. I'm really stubborn about it. I'm not about to race in something I feel uncomfortable in.

The LZR is what feels good and fast for me and that's what I'm sticking to. Also, I hate how long the new bodysuits take to put on. The issue being discussed is how much polyurethane is in a suit and what difference that can make to speed - but for me comfort and an open back are paramount. Anything that constricts me (and is likely to split) down the back is not going to work for me. I'm told that the 2009 super-suits will 'make me faster', but I feel they will make me slower relative to the size of gain others might get.

Later that day, as the sun sinks and shadows return, I feel a little flatter than I did this morning. I watch as Anastasia breaks the world record and takes away my European mark in 58.48sec in the semi-final just before mine. Courtesy of the suits, the world record count is mounting like never before and will reach 43 by the end of the eight days of racing. Because I've chosen to stay in the LZR I wore last year, I have no doubt that swimming inside 59sec marks progress in my swimming speed. I stay focused and swim 58.74, another British record and inside the world record that had stood until Anastasia's effort. I feel good, get to bed and sleep soundly.

CHAPTER 20

Gold! WR! And Catharsis

"Sometimes things become possible if we want them bad enough"

– T.S. ELIOT

The day of the 100m backstroke final dawns. At the pool for the evening session, a steady stream of people flow past to wish me well as I lie on the bench getting a massage from Pat Dunleavy. I'm so happy but so nervous all at the same time; all the appeals for me to "stay calm" are not helping me to stay calm at all. I'm overstimulated. My heart is in my mouth but I also have a sense of limitless energy in every muscle. I'm ready to race but I have to wait. Anticipation only enhances the tension.

There's a place between peace and energy generating anxiety that creates the perfect feeling of balance that athletes need when getting ready to race at peak. I settle in the right place: not too nervous that I'm going to be sick but just on the edge of that feeling.

I exchange a few last words with Wilby and it's off to the "call room", the "ready room", the place where we all gather beyond a suit check and before walking out on to the burning deck and the starting blocks. This is my sanctuary. I'm in a good place. I chat to my teammate and friend Lizzie Simmonds. We've shared a lot of experience, chatted to each other about everything under the sun. Here we are again, nattering, relaxed but focused. Most others are quiet. They're not having fun. They're struggling with the moment instead of enjoying it.

Positive energy flows through me in waves; the kind that you can harness to best effect when you know you've put the hard graft in. I've been hugely disciplined and dedicated in training. I now take pride in the pain I've gone through to get to this moment. Such thoughts and the certainty in them are massive: if your confidence is in the right place you can achieve everything and anything. Expectation no longer weighs on me: there may be a lot of people I'm trying to please but there's only one I need to answer to: me.

We're called out to our race. Anastasia Zueva, the Russian and fastest seed, is in lane 4; I'm in 5, so I walk out to the blocks right behind her. She's shaking her arms, getting ready to race. I can see in her eyes that she is deeply nervous. She looks at me and I look back, smiling, and wish her "good luck". It catches her off guard. She was in "the zone", that pre-race place of singular focus - and I've taken her out of it.

As I glance down the length of the pool, I feel plugged in. This is my moment. The place is crackling with energy, sun, shade, sparkling water, warm breeze. I'm home. She's here. I look skyward and murmur "this one's for you, Mum".

I feel her presence. It feels different to how I felt last year. I'm no longer grieving. I'm no longer using raw emotion and pain to drive me. Instead, I feel the strength that she has given me in my life, the gift of a great childhood, the love and devotion that she bestowed on me. This feeling will live with me all my days; her strength on top of mine.

Buoyed by that fleeting thought, I feel as though I'm on autopilot for the race. I know I have done what it will take, know I have gone through the routine of stretches, massage and the things that work for me to be at my best. I have stuck to my path. I'm on top of the world and know I have something good to bring out of me.

Only later will I appreciate how the race panned out. In the throes of battle, I have no idea that I'm behind at the turn. Pushing off the wall for the second of two lengths, it feels like a switch has been flicked. I know that I have an amazing second 50m and it's time to bring my kick into gear, to drive for home like never before, to grit my teeth, to shut out pain and finish the race in the most efficient and precise way possible. Hundredths of a second can make the difference between gold and no medal at all.

I hit the wall, look up at the scoreboard right down the other end of the pool and soak up the result: 58.12sec, a world-record victory 0.06sec ahead of Anastasia. Relief washes over me. I am so excited, the energy from Mum still present. She's right here with me. I'm so happy, not just with the result but because I want her to be in this moment, to be a part of it - and I feel she is. Looking back, I will struggle to dissect each intense feeling but here and now, immediately after the race, every emotion imaginable seems to rush through me, intense, storm-like.

The gauntlet of TV cameras, broadcasters, press and the media conference is something of a blur. There are a lot of questions about suits ("mine is the same as in 2008, so I know I've made great progress") and about Mum. I try to explain that I had not consciously set out to think of her as I looked skyward before the race; I just had a strong sense of the strength I get from her. Her soul is still present in the world. It is not easy to explain. I feel as though her spirit and strength are alive in me.

There is a spiritual side to me. I don't expect others to impose their beliefs on me and I don't impose mine on them but I do believe that everything happens for a reason. I hate having this thought but the fact that my Mum died has helped me to win a world title. Events have forced me to deal with it - and proven that I can. Although I don't know it here and now in Rome, her death will come to help me deal with further sorrows that await me.

I wouldn't be the person I am without life having played out the way it has. These joyful days in Rome are charged with the positive energy from all that has happened. Barely a day goes by, of course, without me wishing Mum was still here with us in person. I'm aware that some pity me. They say "it must be so hard for you". It is but I don't seek pity, particularly not in the spotlight I find myself under.

Even private moments are anything but. The anti-doping agent awaits me at the end of the race. I sign a form to say I consent to drugs testing, obligatory if you set a world record or if you're picked out at random. The chaperone who stays by my side every second until I'm delivered to the anti-doping suite speaks only Italian. I misunderstand when she offers to hold my cap and goggles. Turns out she wants a souvenir. The last time I see her is the last time I will see the cap and goggles I raced to gold in.

Once the door to the anti-doping room closes, there is a familiar process to go through, including sitting waiting to pee while the officer, watching everything I do, chats to me. It can be off-putting having someone watch you pee but I've got used to it and most officers know that when I go quiet, I'm ready to go - and they should be quiet too. All part of the catalogue of amusing memories down the years, along with the stranger who has my golden cap and goggles.

Next to the funny file of my career there's also a book of special moments. Those include the first time I see Wilby after the race. He is standing on the deck in the warm-down pool where the walls are garlanded with stunning mosaics built in Romanesque splendour for the pleasure of Mussolini. I run up to my coach, my guide, and give him a massive hug. Tears of joy well in his eyes.

It has always been this way. He cares how we all do. He has been a father figure to me. Wilby was the one who sent me home to see Mum, who made sure I made it in time. He's been through everything with me, was always there if things went wrong. He worked on training sets that were specifically designed with me in mind to help me to get the very best out of myself. He took pride in that work.

His dedication, his devotion never let up, through thick and thin. He's steered me in the right direction and I've placed great store in the advice he's given to me when I've had to speak to the media at difficult times. He has brought things out in me that I would have concealed for fear of not knowing how to express myself. He's shown me to look at the horizon, consider the wider picture, explain how I feel, show the warmth in me, warmth that he made me aware of.

In Rome, he is part of a huge support network. From the moment I leave the pool at the end of the race, there's someone I know waving at me, smiling, cheering, congratulating me. There are Brits in the crowd, the stands and the warm-down pool and up in the swell of faces as I walk along the deck after the medal ceremony I see people I know from Florida.

There's Puerto Rican Corale Lopez, a member of our sprint freestyle group. She's standing with Felipe, another teammate and a man I've been close to, smiling down at me, both waving. One of the great things about being a Gator is that, come the big meet, there are people on squads from all over the world there supporting you as though we were all back in Gainesville, one big family. Wilby is actually coach to the Cayman Islands here at the championships. I feel an amazing sense of support from everywhere. My Dad is in the crowd and everywhere I look I see my Gator family, my Britain team family.

Back at the team hotel, we hold our daily meeting. My success is celebrated but the memory of that moment will fade faster than my recollection of meetings back in Beijing at the Olympic Games. Then, the theme was 'good, but disappointing too'. The harder edge is the one you remember most keenly. It was important to maintain a good attitude at the Games and we did that even when the chips were down. We had so many near misses in 2008 and the tension of that time lives on in me.

Many a happy moment in Rome will become blurred in time, in part because I'm so very happy anyway and largely because the gold medal, while something I've been striving for all my life, is not as important for me personally as it is for those who support me. For them it is the thing that counts; for me it is the key that unlocks the real reward, happiness.

I don't like to stand out, even at times like these. Back at base after the race, I walk into the dining room and deliberately sit in the same place I've sat in all week long. I try to bring a sense of normality to the evening, talk about things I would have talked about anyway. I just want to be me with people and have them be themselves with me. I'm uncomfortable as the centre of attention and steer the conversation away from me. I don't want to talk about the fact that I just won a gold medal.

The championships are not over. I have more work to do. I want to keep doing the things I've been doing. I've had spaghetti and meat sauce every day because it is bland and I feel fine on it. I also eat bread with Nutella, my only chocolate fix, apart from the one bar I allow myself when I get back to the room with Jemma Lowe after the 100m final and we open the Pandora's box we call a fridge. It's full of the good stuff. To finally savour chocolate, job done, is the happiest of feelings ever! At least that's what we agree as we scoff.

Jemma mentions my swim just once. She says 'wow, that was so good, amazing' - and then we go back to our normal routine. There is so much more to our friendship that it is easy to talk about anything other than my success. Besides, she still has to race - and we don't want to talk swimming. She falls asleep but I'm still buzzing. I'm so excited. A million thoughts flow through my mind before I'm able to drift off.

The 200m goes well. I finish fourth, the worst place but a good result for me. I explain to the media, for the first time, why I think that the curse of fourth (twice in Beijing, once here) visits me so often: my name is "Spof-Fourth". I know I could be really good over 200m if I ever learnt to swim it properly. The truth is, I'm not good enough at making myself hurt at the beginning of the race and I'm too far out of touch by the end of the race to have the same impact as I do over 100m.

The next fourth place hurts more: the medley relay. Fran Halsall has a silver in the 100m freestyle but the other two girls, Ellen Gandy and Lowri Tynan, have no medal. We want one for them. The leadership skills that I've developed on college teams, where the standard can vary from good club swimmers to world-class athletes, are not needed in the same way here. I do what I can to keep us together and happy but these girls know what's required. I'm just so happy to be around people who are so good at what they do. In world-class waters, that is not always good enough. Fourth. It feels good to know I touched ahead of everyone again on the opening 100m backstroke.

The next morning I have a photoshoot at the Trevi Fountain and we all get time to explore this amazing city. It's a great and rare day off, with a tour of the Vatican and St Peter's and a bus ride around Rome. After the shoot, I have lunch with Becky Adlington and Jo Jackson. Both are inspirational, down-to-earth, friendly. Olympic medal winners, they are also people who I've grown to love and cherish.

Come the evening I'm with a different crew and ready to party. Those of us who are based in America and are not funded from home get to go out. Felipe is there too. We drink, dance, we get messy and only make it back to the hotel the next day - just in time to pack and make the flight. It's almost a release mechanism at the end of a big meet. After a year of dedication and complete focus in the pool, limited drinking, limited partying, letting go and having fun are part of the climb back down to normality.I love it that swimming is bigger than me and bigger than elite sport. A psychologist once told me that if your heart is in the right place you can create determination and motivation in others. It is very important for me that anything we achieve is for our country and its people, something that binds us.

The pool is kind of a cage but you can experience everything outside that cage and make the experience so much bigger than just the one race, one moment. Ripples from that bigger moment flow into many areas of life. That, and not the gold medal, is what I will take with me into life after Rome.

Before returning home to Florida, there's a difficult day to face in England.

As we drive in silence down the winding roads towards the cemetery in Otley, I still hear that chink of metal handles on wood that struck me on a cold day after Olympic trials almost 18 months ago. I feel like I'm having another out-of-body experience. It's as if I'm looking down on the scene from far above the rolling green hills around us. Mum's sister, Margaret, her husband Hugh, my brother Peter and our Dad are here too, their presence comforting but strangely remote.

We arrive at her final resting place, one she shares with other members of the family: she would be happy to be here in these glorious hills, a part of this spectacular setting. I glance heavenwards and cement the image in my mind of her in this place of gentle breeze, blue skies dotted with fluffy white clouds, hilltops of green and yellow, distant houses lining the horizon.

The sketch of that day, that snapshot in time, will live deep in my mind to the end of my days, as will an overwhelming, deep sense of contentment. I feel her looking down on me, I feel her in my bones, in my soul. Her happiness feeds mine. Tears cascade down my face, each droplet a gentle reminder that I can grieve, that what I feel is "normal", is to be expected at such times. Even so, I'm not quite ready to let go.

Suppressing the urge to break down and fall to my knees under the weight of sorrow, I look at the horizon, take in the hills, welcome the breeze and place all of it in a special room in my heart, one I can go to when I need to find strength.You believed in me Mum.It is a cathartic moment, a milestone in my healing.

On the cusp of a world title and world record in the 100m backstroke in Rome, 2009, I look skyward and murmur "this one's for you, Mum"

Me and mum, my rock, 2006, the year before she left this world

Graduation Day! From the left, Elizabeth Kemp; Coach Gregg Troy; Stephanie Proud; Coach Martyn Wilby; Me and my first roommate at college, Kristen Beales

Can you spot me? Twelfth in from the left, top row, with Great Britain teammates on our pre-World Championships camp in Sardinia in 2009

At the Trevi Fountain in Rome after winning the world title in 2009

"The Eternal City. It is electrifying to be here. Rome is full of shadows, metaphoric and real. History at every corner, every turn of the head. The buildings, the structures, the living canvas of sharply contrasting yellow light and deep shadow that sweeps and transforms the city, gives me a sense of the spiritual, the beautiful, the spectacular. I feel welcome, there is a warmth here, I feel the presence of the people of this place and the monumental events that unfolded here."

My support team included the kids I teach to
swim at the Gators in Gainesville, Florida

"Somewhere down the line of learning, a switch is flicked and an arm will come out of the water and swing across the surface. It's their first stroke as a swimmer. A light goes on. To be there at the dawn of skill and tell a child how well they've done fills me with energy."

The Great Britain Olympic swimming team the day after selection in March 2012 on the deck at the London Aquatics Centre

Light relief after the swimming was done at the Olympic Games, with Britain teammates - from left, Ellen Gandy, Me, Georgia Davies and Jemma Lowe

Fun and Games: time to party at the Closing Ceremony in London, August 2012

New horizons: me and my brother Peter in Red Rock Canyon, New Year, 2013 at the start of the next chapter

The Crisis Center

"People are just as wonderful as sunsets if you let them be. When I look at a sunset, I don't find myself saying, "Soften the orange a bit on the right hand corner." I don't try to control a sunset. I watch it in awe as it unfolds"

— CARL ROGERS

The start of a new semester is the catalyst for a new start in my life. Not only am I back in classes and back swimming after a glorious three-week holiday but the role of captain grants me the chance once more to lead a team of spectacular young ladies and help to steer them to the best of their abilities. I'm the women's captain, Roberto Gomez the men's captain.

Apparently, we won the vote hands down, gaining the lion's share of support from swimmers and coaches alike. We will spend our final year of eligibility for college swimming, under amateur rules, at the University of Florida learning about leadership. Roberto's approach is one that I envy and support wholeheartedly. His clear direction and vocal enthusiasm for the team inspires me. It takes confidence (and spreads confidence) for a leader to step back and allow people to shine and show their own skills as a way of getting them to go in the right direction. Roberto does that with aplomb.

The calibre of the team leaves me feeling unequal to the task. Yes, I have a world record now, and I've travelled to other countries on four continents, which speaks volumes in a place where half of the team doesn't have a passport, home the only place they've known. But no, I don't feel as though I fit as captain. It isn't who I am, or at least it's not who I was.

In my mind, I am no longer just Gemma; I have been placed on a pedestal. I am now a role model, a perception that makes me uncomfortable. I try so hard to revert back to the girl who was always striving and never happy with what she had achieved. Now achievement has started to feel like a burden. The pressure to live up to the expectations of team and coaches is suffocating.

Against that backdrop, I embrace more stress as I take up the gruelling task of training at the Alachua County Crisis Center. I'd become interested in the power of helping myself by helping others after talking to Jay in the wake of the Beijing Olympic Games about his own voluntary work.

A six-week training programme, my new lessons in life take up two nights a week for three hours at a time. It's full on. I start to transform myself into a phone counsellor for suicide intervention and learn what it takes to sit in someone else's most vulnerable moments, to be given the privilege of sharing with someone their weakest and darkest seconds, minutes and sometimes hours. Role play after role play we live out real-life situations. I learn what I would need to say to someone who may or may not attempt to take their own life while speaking to me down the phone or soon after ending the call.

Six weeks training is an energy sapping commitment. I can't really pinpoint what has driven me to want to do this other than a memory of my own overwhelming ache and struggle in the face of all-consuming grief on a single night of complete darkness. I get through it but it comes back to haunt me in the form of a kind of mirror-image spectre of myself who asks "why me?"

It leads me to want to help others who find themselves in a momentary or constant state of pain.

There are 50 of us at the first session. By the sixth week of training there will be just 12 of us left, the weeding-out process keeping everyone on their toes. I want this passionately. I plunge deep into an experience that turns out to be amazing: I sense myself maturing from a mediocre listener and friend to an empathetic listener with acquired skills that will stay with me for the rest of my life.

As I learn, I forgive myself for succumbing to the four "modes of response" that have negative consequences when it comes to effective communication with those in crisis: giving advice, interpreting, supporting and probing. I focus instead on paraphrasing, active listening and allowing my client the space to be themselves, unique and complete. I'm beginning to understand that the naive me of the past, the girl who thought of herself as a good listener capable of helping people, is only just learning how to truly understand the person in crisis.

The biggest change I need to make is to avoid switching the conversation to me; to avoid turning someone else's problem into my language but rather adapt my language to their problem. I learn that it's never about me. Although I am writing this book and it is all about me and my experience and you are reading it on that basis, it is not about me. It's about you and your experiences, your life and how my experience might help you to relate to your own journey.

Talking about what I have been through is not the way to go when speaking to anyone whose problem leaves them struggling at the bottom of the well, suffocating in their own terror, lost in the emotional fog of their crisis. Telling them what to do and how to get there will not help them: it will simply exacerbate the disorientation that has left them feeling isolated and buried at the bottom of the deepest, darkest pit of solitude.

The way to go, I'm taught, is to jump into the well with them, to effectively sit beside the person in crisis and feel what they are feeling. To say that the good listener should suffocate with the person in need of help may sound surreal; how can anything that puts two people in a place of emotional crisis be seen as anything other than bizarre? Yet this is the only way you can truly empathise with someone, truly connect with the person who needs you to connect with them.

The crisis intervention training is gruelling but intriguing. On the first day, I sit in a room full of complete strangers but feel I belong. I'm nervous, confused, excited and inquisitive all at once. I make many new friends and leave with a sense of accomplishment. I'm determined - but fearful too.

During the course of these six weeks of crisis training, I also have my 'normal' regime in the pool, school and I travel to competitions. It's almost business as usual, except that Tuesdays and Thursdays are three hours longer and my head is full of fresh thoughts.

Sitting here in crisis class among these compassionate people, I'm learning more about myself than I ever felt possible. My brain and my emotions are being stretched. It feels good. I gain a deeper understanding of empathy, listening and authority skills. I've been transformed by the past six weeks of intensive focus. I have purpose and meaning. It is almost as if each fibre of my being has been unstitched and sewn back more evenly. I get to grips with what it takes to calm an escalating crisis, to talk about suicide openly, to talk about taboo issues openly. Most of all, I find a place of non-judgmental calm within me, a place that allows the person in crisis to express their deepest fears, reveal their secret pain. It's such an honour to be with someone in their darkest moments.

The training flies by quickly and concludes with graduation to the phone. I'm exhausted, satisfied and proud of what we've achieved as I celebrate six weeks of renewal with my new friends. I text Wilby: ". graduation onto the phone lines as a certified crisis phone line counsellor is the most satisfying and gratifying accomplishment of my life, more so than making the Olympic team, more so than breaking the World Record. I have found something to call my own, something that will provide satisfaction".

I'm on a high. But low is never far away. I don't see it coming: sadness is creeping over me. It sets in slowly and ties you down long before you realise what's happening. How, I ask myself, can I be a "crisis counsellor" if I'm sunk in my own crisis?

I've had an incredible journey with a group of fresh people in my life but here I am questioning friendships old and new, regarding them as fake and unworthy of my time. I long for someone to provide for me what I try so hard to provide for others: my cries for help seem never to be answered. I need to find those answers for myself. I don't understand my feelings: my life is so great, I'm so lucky and yet I'm overwhelmed by sadness and negative thought that leads me into a cul-de-sac of anti-social, self-imposed isolation.

Every time I grasp for the lifeline that I think relationships with men provide for me, I cannot connect emotionally. It feels like I'm the cowboy lassoing his horse but then strangling it before it has a chance to settle down, to find its footing, to come close.

People ask me if I'm ok but what I hear is 'I don't really care, I don't really have time to listen but I thought I should ask anyway because you appear to have got yourself stuck in a hole'.

I tell myself: tomorrow will be a better day, I will enjoy the company of my friends, I will provide myself with something happy to think about and to do and I will not allow myself to sink further into the emptiness that has engulfed me this past week.

Questions of family ties and independence occupy my thoughts: Dad has his life; he doesn't need me but he jumps on any chance to control me; without that control he feels he is worthless in my life. Do your homework, train hard, speak to this paper, email this fan; he is controlling my time, like

I actually have some. And when he's not doing all of that he's invisible, has nothing to contribute. The arguments in my head are the kind that can spill over into real conflict. I dread the thought of calling him, just in case. How can I miss someone so much and yet not want to call or speak to them or just let them know I love them?

I call him. There's no answer. It feels like I'm in a game of phone tag, each unanswered call adding another layer to the depression unfolding in me. It occurs to me that avoiding what I've framed in my mind as "arguments" is actually something else: I am trying not to stare at the void left by Mum. She had the gift of unconditional love; the intuition to know when I would call; she took time to talk, no matter what it was that I had to say; she knew exactly when to call me because she knew exactly what I was doing and when I would be doing it, it seems to me.

That rock-solid place of comfort and understanding has been gone for almost two years. It is a month shy of her death, I'm on the cusp of my 22nd birthday this month of November and I am still nursing the hole in my heart. It is long past the time when I should have moved on, got past the mourning, this great loss in my life, found closure. Isn't it?

My heavy heart continues to be a burden on others and a hindrance in my life. It limits my potential to be what I imagine a role model might be: someone who has everything they ever wanted or needed. The utter despair that continues to wash over me even at times of happiness has built a wall between me and those who love me and those I might know better were it not for the invisible force that separates us.

I feel disgusted with myself. I am so sick of settling for a physical connection with someone because I am terrified of deeper emotion. Keep trucking and you will find a way to the road, I keep telling myself. All the while I see storms gathering on the wind out to sea, heading landwards to make the road impassable. I cannot allow myself to fill the void left by Mum with men. The risk is too high. What if I lose them too? I don't think my heart is strong enough to handle that.

Thoughts tumble in all directions: I know what I must do; I know that I cannot sleep with Felipe again; I know that it still crosses my mind that I might sleep with him again; I know I still fantasise about him; I know I will look to see if he has written on my Facebook wall to wish me a happy birthday; I don't care; at least, I don't want to care, but I think that I do. I want this to be something I can hold on to, to prove to myself that I can do just that.

For a moment, I come back to the place that grounds me: I am me; I know me; I am better than this and I just haven't found something or someone who can handle me.

Dealing With It

I lurch back to a time soon after Mum's death. It occurs to me that Jay has inspired me to do all this. He has been through so much but he is still an Olympic medallist, he became a firefighter and he is also a crisis volunteer. He advocates volunteerism. I'm not doing what I'm doing for him but I did take this path because of him. Its changed my world and I'm eternally grateful to him for that. Where love fits into that I have no idea.

I miss Mum so much: all I want to do is speak to her and I can't. I know who to ask the questions running through my head but she's not there. I just want that one call in which I hear her say "I know what's going on and you can talk to me about it all. I love you." I love you too Mum.

CHAPTER 22

The Duel and Philip

"Let everything happen to you. Beauty and terror. Just keep going. No feeling is final"

— RAINER MARIA RILKE

I've been living a falsehood. What I will realise somewhere down the line (what I already know deep down) is that no-one and nothing will ever replace what my mother gave me, what she was to me and what she is to me. The closest I will ever come to bridging the gap is what I have had all along: family, Wilby, the Gators, my friends, the myriad people who come into my life and contribute to me making the most of it and getting the best out of myself.

In contrast to those times when I fall deep into self-doubt and believe that nobody wants to be around me, I've always felt a deep sense of being loved and have known, without wishing to sound conceited, that people feel comfortable around me. That means more to me than any success in the pool. I like to have people around me feel safe, be at ease in my presence.

True friendship is like that. It endures change and absence and transcends status, be that 'world champion' or anything else.

It's why I love to meet up with old friends in England at least once a year when we can renew connections to a happy childhood.

Come Christmas 2009, a very special year is drawing to a close and I'm home in England for business and pleasure. A European "All-Stars" team has been selected to take on a strong USA squad at the Duel in the Pool in Manchester on the eve of the festive break.

The Americans have come looking for the win - and they get it, by quite a sizeable margin. Into the bargain, six more world records fall in two days at what is our last meet of the year and the last at which we will race in non-textile suits. A January 1, 2010, ban looms for apparel that set the clock on fast-forward.

On the last night of racing, I swim the 100m backstroke and finish third. It's the two-year anniversary of Mum's death and it plays on my mind. I'm not quite the emotional wreck I thought I was going to be but I feel raw, my heart heavy, my mind racing in a lane of its own.

It has been the same each and every anniversary, each birthday, every Mother's Day. I expect that cycle of emotions to always be there and look to those dates in a positive way too, each also a welcome reminder of the time we had, of the life Mum had.

A year ago, we enjoyed the distraction of New York at a time when everything was still so raw. That visit to the Big Apple helped to keep sorrow at bay. We're staying home this year and, the Duel done, I head south to meet up with friends who have meant a lot to me for as long as I can recall.

Philip was the first person I had a strong emotional connection with before my Mum got cancer and before any of the events that have shaped my life these past few years. We were 16 going on 17. Our relationship was immature. He was really into cars and taught me how to drive like a complete maniac. He introduced me to the world of boys and what it means to be in a relationship with a guy.

Philip swam for Fareham Nomads not too far from my own club, Portsmouth Northsea. I fell for him almost straight away and lost my virginity just three weeks after we started going out. The relationship did not last long. In fact, the act out of the way, he told me he still had feelings for his ex-girlfriend and felt bad about what he'd done. He was my first - and my first heartbreak: he really hurt me and it took a lot to trust again. To this day, I have yet to trust anyone fully because of that first experience. It was the kind of mistake a 16-17-year-old makes and has to live with.

Since then, Philip has been in and out of my life because we share some of the same friends. There is always tension between us. After the World Championships in Rome, I held a big party back home in England. Philip was there. We felt a connection but he had a girlfriend at the time. We did some stupid things and people noticed. At some point we drifted up to the attic where I'd built and installed several beds when I was younger. He sat down next to me and poured out his feelings: I really wish I hadn't hurt you in the first place; I really wish you lived in England and we could make something work but nothing ever works out because you're always in a different country and something always gets in the way. He was very loyal to his girlfriend; nothing happened and that was that. Philip's girlfriend heard a whisper, though, and she was hurt.

Four months later, here I am back in Britain for Christmas at the house of Dad's new love. I'd known about June White for almost a year, ever since Dad had plucked up the courage to tell me about her. We don't talk all that often during the year but over the course of a week or so back in January, he'd called me constantly and he was really starting to frustrate me because I kept thinking 'why is he calling if he's got nothing to say'.

He could sense I was annoyed and that probably made it all the harder for him to say what he'd wanted to say. Finally, at end of the week, he called and told me that he had a girlfriend. My first reaction was: "Dad! Is that what you've been trying to tell me all week?!" Then I told him how happy I was to hear his news, not least of all because of the distance between us. It was not like I could keep popping round to see how he was doing. I needed to know he was happy and happy with someone.

I didn't suffer the adverse reaction so common when "another woman" arrives on the scene. I was just really happy that he was not in a rut and had found someone to fill the space. It let me know he was ok, that he had someone to look out for him. We rarely spoke about it after that.

Sometimes, the silence of what never gets said leaves room for confusion. I see Philip in the days leading up to Christmas. He's single again. I'm staying with a friend in Portsmouth about 45 minutes from our house so that I can go out partying. It also gives me somewhere to go back to and that alone will help me to avoid going off with him again and starting the whole cycle up again.

Philip has told friends of mine that he had always liked me, that he'd wished he'd never hurt me and wished there was a chance of patching things up. That thought is racing through my mind when, with considerable trepidation, I find myself opposite him on the dance floor on Christmas Eve. I feel stronger than I have ever been yet there is still a lot of sexual tension between us. Add a drop of wine to weaken my resolve and that old longing returns with a vengeance.

Philip's friends are all in couples: Nick and Chloe, Chris and Claire and here we are, at a comfortable distance but in danger of getting closer once again. He is drunk and I have never been able to say 'no'. We start to dance closer, his gorgeous brown eyes looking into mine, the wine and want in him obvious. After what we've been through together, I feel I can read him. A slow song later and I'm in his arms but the tempo picks up and we separate.

All of a sudden, I hear an inner voice: not this time. I have the urge to run, to go and find my school friends, a different clique around the corner. I see my escape route: my friend and saviour Anna and her house, a haven that will allow me to break the cycle at last.

I make a mumbled excuse and leave him on the dance floor. It is a very conscious decision, a moment of clarity, a turning point, the start of saying 'no'. A conversation I had with Wayne, the psychologist, back in the summer, springs to mind: "...you can say 'no' - and that's ok".

It's not just with boys, I almost never say no to anyone in any circumstance, especially if someone looks like they're in trouble or needs me. Tonight, I may not have dealt with that aspect of it but I have reached a watershed in my relationships with men.

I feel relieved, another positive step taken in a year full of them - with one more to come.

Chapter 23

Christmas at June's

"Without a family, man, alone in the world, trembles with the cold"

— ANDRE MAUROIS

We're spending Christmas at June White's beautiful farmhouse. It's in the country about 10 minutes from our place. She's the new love in Dad's life and she has a large and complicated family. Her daughter Vicky is there with her husband Craig and their son; Vicky and Sharon are June's daughters from her first marriage; her second husband Tony, died of cancer, and four kids call June "Mum" but she's not their birth mother.

My brother Peter and I have never had a Christmas like this one, with so many people gathered as one huge family. The chaos and excitement wrap around me and make me feel whole again.

They all get drunk and there's lots of laughter. June is amazing: her own disjointed family has shaped her into a woman who understands the nuance of altered relationships.

She's loading the dishwasher and I'm staring out of the window. She asks me to sit down for a minute and says: "Look, I've been through this before and I don't want to step on your toes. I need you to tell me if I do anything to step on your toes or your Mum's toes, even if it comes down to parking my car in your Mum's garage. If that isn't ok with you, you have to tell me - and I won't do it."

We'd met each other before, when June came out to the SEC Championships in the US back in spring but there was never enough time to sit down and be "normal". This Christmas is our first chance to get to know each other and communication is open from the start. She has put herself out of her comfort zone and in doing that has created an amazing relationship between us.

Communication is really important to me but it is something I really struggle with. I advocate solid and clear lines of communication but if I have to sit down and initiate an uncomfortable conversation with the potential for conflict, it can be a chore, to say the least, especially if I have something to say that may be uncomfortable for the person sitting opposite me. I hate the idea of saying anything that's going to hurt someone's feelings. Its almost impossible for me to do. I'm much better at writing my thoughts down in a letter or an email.

I'm immensely grateful to June for being frank and straightforward. I notice lots of comparisons between her and my Mum too: unique in so many ways, of course, but they both loved strawberries; the way June nags my Dad reminds me of Mum; their personalities are strong and independent; there's even something very similar in the way they cut their hair.

June is packing up all her stuff in between the festive fun: she's moving in with Dad after Christmas. I watch them flirting, joking around with each other. Before Christmas, June had asked Dad, tongue in cheek, if he was going to get her a diamond. He bought her a huge plastic joke gem. We've all got silly hats on. Dad's is a turkey. There's a child-like joy about Dad and June and seeing it brings me hope and happiness. Their upbeat mood is catching and I love being around them.

I'm in a new world and I have a sense of relief and renewal: these new family members of mine are like the petrol that's making the car run again. June is a really engaging person: she doesn't push for information, she hasn't tried to be my Mum, she hasn't forced a relationship on me. She's made it easy for us to talk to each other. We feel free in each other's company.

I have another secret joy this Christmas. Emily, June's little granddaughter reminds me of me when I was younger and I spend a lot of time playing silly games with her. I'm not only seeing Dad's relationship with June blossom but this blonde child I'm having so much fun with has transported me back to my own happy days of innocence.

By the time I get back to the US after Christmas, my mood is brighter than it's been in what feels like a very long time. I know Dad is ok, that June is living with him and looking after him. I no longer need to worry. A weight has lifted.

My College Swansong

"Remember that sometimes not getting what you want is a wonderful stroke of luck"

— DALAI LAMA XVI

Back home in Gainesville, I get straight back into the happy time I've been having since the autumn when focus shifted to the college swim season. It's my senior year, the end to my college career, and I'm captain of the women's team. I could become the first woman in NCAA history to win the 200-yard backstroke title four years in succession. If I feel the pressure and a weight of expectation, I also have responsibility to lead the way for the whole squad as we prepare for a showdown at Purdue in West Lafayette, Indiana, in March.

I feel good about the way I've been able to lead. During the season I set up a few team bonding activities, connecting the team as a family. Understanding the intrinsic bonds that can help each and everyone of them to grow, together as one and as individuals is a core value of mine. It seems to be working well.

Where there's been any drama, it's been dealt with through me. In other years, most of the drama went through the coaches but this senior class of 2010 is showing its maturity: we've been able to be happy and civil with each other even in cases where people don't actually like each other. We understand the value of working together with respect so that we can achieve the goal we've set for ourselves: victory.

In all my years at college, this is the first year in which I feel that the women's team has enjoyed a truly strong connection. This squad is a unique sorority, one in which each member is able to accept direction from those leading.

The way I've chosen to lead is to set an example, to step back and let everyone else take responsibility and only jump in if and when direction is needed. It helps not to take sides, not to engage in a blame game when a problem arises. Each member of my team has incredible strengths, each athlete has something to offer the team. It is my responsibility to foster an environment in which everyone is heard and everyone has something to contribute.

Take "dry season", the period each year from January 1 to the end of the NCAA championships during which the team does not drink alcohol. I don't drink much or go out partying too often anyway, so it's no great hardship. I think the best way to handle it is to give responsibility to those who do drink and might find it hard going: I put the two girls who do like to drink in control of solidarity by allowing them to set the date beyond which no-one on the team would touch a drop or go out partying.

No sooner have I done so than the two girls who set the cutoff time have broken the rules, a birthday here, a glass of wine there, a night out downtown too. Goodwill breaks down. There's a lot of "she said this and they did that and this happened too".

Embroiling myself in the middle of all the conflict and arguments just feels like wasted energy so I send the whole team an email: We Gators are reigning SEC champions from 2009 - but we're not acting like it. I don't want to know who went out and who didn't go out. I want you all to be responsible for who you are and take on board the fact that we're a team that can win, not just SECs but NCAAs too.

It seems to me that playing peacemaker will benefit my team more than taking sides. Any message would be lost if I start saying "she's right, you're wrong". I'm more likely to get a good response if I say "you're all wrong, so come back and figure it out". I need them to connect, not disconnect. That was the point of the team-building exercise I arranged: I ask each of them to write down a brief line about the positives they see in each of their teammates. In other words, let's look at the good things we've got - because there are a lot of them and they're worth celebrating.

In any group of 20 to 30 girls, there are bound to be disagreements but just keeping that to a miniMum and allowing them to see their teammates as fellow humans and not just another swimmer on the same squad is very important to me.

When the drinks issue comes up, the message I want to get across is simple: do what you can do in the pool to the highest standard you're capable of. Pour your energy into that and drop the damn gossip and all that stuff. It seems to do the trick and the team feels more connected, more focused, with the same call to arms applying to the whole shoal.

It helps to be feeling on top of the world right now, a world record and title behind me, a sense of friendship from the whole squad and a relationship with the coaches built on respect that allows me to go to them if it all gets too much.

The season will end without the need for me to ask for help from the coaches as captain. That's a plus point because trust isn't broken and everyone feels like they're being treated like the adults you're asking them to be, no lingering perception that the captain is telling tales on the team. I'm dealing with teammates who are at a watershed in their lives somewhere between being kids and grown ups.

To serve as team captain is a duty. It demands my full attention and a lot of other things matter less to me for a while. I have a voice, more of a say in things than I've had before and I feel I'm in the perfect place to do a good job. The events of the past couple of years have brought me to an unfamiliar place: I have the confidence to lead.

We arrive in Purdue as a unit. On the first day of battle, I win the 100yds backstroke, make the consolation final of the 200 medley and we win the 4x50 freestyle relay, my split time the fastest at the meet. Things are looking good but conserving energy is a big part of handling a multiple-event programme: not easy when you have three days of frenetic racing - I'm doing four relays and three individuals, heats and finals - with cheerleading on top.

If I'm tired after the first day, I'm exhausted after the second. On the last night, I have a relay and the 200yds backstroke to finish off the meet and my college career.

I will write a line in NCAA history if I win the 200yds backstroke for a fourth time. I race, hit the wall and can't believe what has just happened. Second. I just didn't swim like I knew I should and could have. Frustration and a touch of anger course through me.

Salt is rubbed in my wound when I hear what they're playing over the speakers: "Fields of Gold" by Sting, the same song that always evokes memories of the cancer research adverts that used the tune. "Are you kidding me," a voice inside my head says. "I just lost a race and you're happy to remind me that I lost my mother to cancer too ... thanks". I'm balling my eyes out - and there's a big race still to go.

Our relay quartet is standing behind the starting block in a state of dismay. We're like a shipwreck. Shara is crying because I'm crying and a selection choice made by the coaches means that a third member of the team is crying because she got the slot and her friend didn't. That leaves one of us with dry eyes.

We stand here blubbing while the last diver to go for the Gators wins off the boards. Now, it's down to us. We think we need to finish top 4, maybe top 5, to win the 2010 championship title. No-one seems sure and there's no time find out. Maybe we need top 3? The thing we are certain of is that we need to fight with everything we've got, our last instruction from the coaches: "Just don't get disqualified!"

The race unfolds and tears give way to yelling each other on. The clock stops, the scoreboard screams a "3" for third next to our names. I'm not sure what that means and there's a momentary hush. Suddenly, Shara - who matches me at 6ft - jumps almost a clear 4ft off the ground. She's ecstatic. I'm still really confused. I don't know what's going on.

We all look over at the team on the deck: they're jumping for joy. It finally clicks: we've won NCAAs! This is the first victory for the women Gators since 1982 - and it happened on our watch. All at once, in this soaring moment of joy, everything that has happened, my not winning my 200yds race, all the crying that followed, all the low points, are drowned out.

The success we have earned together is so much bigger than any individual triumph or disappointment. A united team leaps in celebration; we literally jump for joy. We've achieved something as a team. Together, we four in the relay and our teammates now screaming on the deck. It's something way bigger than my world record - because it's not just about me. That shared experience will be the sharpest memory that I take into life from this moment on.

And here's Wilby, tears in his eyes, a man who has put so much effort in but taking time out now to tell me that what I've put into the team cost me the backstroke race and the line in history. He tells me to be proud of myself: I've sacrificed a personal goal so that the team as a whole, me included, could prosper. Win, win.

That message only sinks in later: at first, I'm elated that the team has won, that we pulled together to achieve a great result. But I would be lying if I said that I didn't come into the meet thinking I could be first four-times 200yds winner. The team victory is the cherry and the icing on top of the cake - but I still feel that winning the title would have made it all the sweeter. I fell shy.

That thought will live with me. It's bound too: I'm a competitor - and that means I don't like losing.

Ages later, I hear that my Dad has written a letter of thanks to all those who have helped me. His words touch me deeply and speak to the importance of the support that I have had every step of the way along what at times has been a harder road than I would have wished for myself or anyone else, even though it has made me who I am.

An open letter to the swimming community

(posted on a college website by Mark Spofforth, Gemma's Dad, March 2010).

All of you reading this who are parents will understand the mixed emotions that surround the birth of your first child. Joy, pride, but above all sheer terror at the thought of bringing a new life into the world and having to nurture and protect him or her with very little training in parenthood.

In our case we had an added problem when the doctors went into a little huddle to discuss some issue with our baby which they didn't want to tell us about straight away - that was a nervous time. As it turned out, it wasn't a major difficulty, and a small operation a year or so later sorted it out.

But really quickly you find yourself leaving your child - a daughter in our case - at her first school, and again the terror at entrusting your baby to a teacher that you don't really know leaves you with a physical pain in your stomach.

Things go well, the child begins to flourish and soon shows an aptitude for swimming, so you take her to the local swim club, and soon the local competitions start. Once again your stomach turns somersaults every time she races; our daughter seemed to come second most of the time, so you spend some time counselling as well and urging her to keep going, "One day you'll be a winner if you keep trying".

The local coach spots something in her psyche and offers to give her longer hours, and eventually county/state competitions become part of the routine, leading to a trip to a national championships and a space on the national talent development team, which in turn lead in our case to a European Junior Competition, and a Gold medal. When the national anthem plays and you daughter stand on the podium, it's impossible not to cry.

A few years on and things are not so good. A really unpleasant illness has kept her out of the water, she's unfit and the national team have pretty much discarded her. Thoughts turn to academic achievements and potential jobs rather than sporting excellence. The illness appears to have been properly diagnosed, but might recur, who knows?

But then we have to choose a University, and we start to think about what it might be like to get away from all the local pressure, and look at the facilities on offer in the USA. Eventually she's offered a golden chance to train at the

University of Florida on a sporting scholarship, even if the Coach thinks this is the riskiest scholarship he's ever awarded, and is daunted by the task ahead trying to get this girl fit... but again, he sees some spark, some character that he thinks might just turn into something given a following wind.

4 years later, and that girl is a World Champion, a World Record Holder, an Olympian, and her last act for the University is to lead her team to the NCAA Championship.

I am so proud of Gemma, but can't forget that fear of the unknown the day she was born, and the days that we've entrusted her on to teachers and coaches who have all paid back that trust with exceptional effort and skill, far beyond what might be expected of an employer.

So I just wanted to say THANKYOU to everyone who has supported her over the last four years, especially the "Gator family".

- *Thankyou to her friends and housemates for accepting a foreigner and helping her understand your country, especially the Beales family, who were there from the first day.*
- *Thankyou to Coaches Troy and Wilby for their coaching skill and their ability to keep Gemma focused when times were really bad - and believe me there were some bad times*
- *Thankyou to UF for understanding the benefits of bringing in foreigners to work and play alongside your students - I understand the debates about the wisdom of doing that, and I hope that you never succumb to those that would have you restrict your tuition to US nationals alone*
- *Thankyou to all the other swimming parents for acting as surrogate parents at swim meets when we were the other side of the world*
- *Thankyou to all the volunteer officials and managers who make the meets possible in the first place*
- *Thankyou to the USA for having a system that has helped make my daughter a World Champion. But most of all Thankyou to the sport that she loves and which has helped build character and confidence into what was once a small and sickly newborn baby. You should all be proud of your part in this success*

Queens of Europe

"The purpose of life is to live it, to taste experience to the utmost, to reach out eagerly and without fear for newer and richer experience"

— E LEANOR R OOSEVELT

The comedown from the grand finale for the Gators in my senior year, the NCAA title at the end of my college swimming days, leaves me feeling like I've hit the ground with no energy left to bounce back up.

Even so, I plough on in training as focus shifts to a tricky international long-course (Olympic, 50m pool) 2010 summer season ahead. Britain has decided to make the Commonwealth Games, in India come October, a priority for each home nation, mine being England. In the middle of it all are the European Championships in August in Budapest, the beautiful Hungarian capital where the competition pool has been on Margaret Island for the best part of a century.

I'm looking forward to it: back in 2006, when the Europeans were last held there, I was recovering from pancreatitis and I sat home with Mum hearing news about a massive electrical storm that wiped the championships out one evening. I recall watching 15-year-old Lizzie Simmonds and the experienced Katy Sexton miss the cut for the final of the 100m backstroke for Britain and wondering what might have been if I hadn't fallen ill.

All of which feels like a very remote memory now as I prepare to leave Gainesville for Europe with Wilby. Although I'm not in the kind of shape I'd been in for Rome world titles last year, we both feel that the residual effects of the level of training I've been doing for so long will carry me through. The three goals, despite the Commonwealth priority later in the year, are straightforward: stay positive, have fun - and get the gold in the 100m.

The first two are what make the third possible and it helps enormously to be surrounded by people who are in the same frame of mind. In Budapest, Lizzie and I are determined to have a ball. While others, heads down and avoiding eye contact, look very serious indeed, we're to be found whacking up the music and performing an Irish jig together in the "call room" before racing. We feel empowered, on top of the world, invincible.

It helps to know that in Europe, if we perform reasonably close to best, the others will have to make big gains to beat us, me over 100m and Lizzie over 200m. It's different when China, Australia, the US and others are not there. When the world gathers, you know you're facing the mother of all swimming battles.

Here on Margaret Island, there is no one to intimidate us, we approach our races knowing we can win, we are confident in our abilities. Expectation at this level is not an issue because it comes from within and is balanced by matching confidence. Expectation is only a problem when it's external, unrealistic and, therefore, exceeds your internal confidence. In this environment, the more confident we feel, the more fun we have, the more likely it is that the result will be the best it can be.

On the second day of racing, Lizzie scorches her way to a debut international senior crown in the 200m and I take the silver. It's the first Brit 1-2 among women at the European long-course showcase since 1958, when Judy Grinham and Margaret Edwards took top honours in the 100m backstroke.

I will end my career never really having got to grips with how to race the 200m. I'm the faster 100m swimmer, but Lizzie has the confidence and understanding to take the 200m out hard enough to set the pace - and hold on. The splits tell me after the race that I was making good gains on Lizzie down the last length. Too late. It's silver for me, Lizzie on 2mins 07.04sec, to my 2:08.25. The next best is more than two seconds away.

It's incredibly special to get a Brit 1-2 and share the podium with a team-mate and friend. A little disheartening too to get beaten by Lizzie but my mind turns to the 100m almost the moment the 200m race is done.

Two days on and I feel like it's my turn for gold, though I have some lingering doubts: am I really ready for it? The mind plays tricks on you at such times: I'm not fully rested - do I have it in me?. My confidence could be higher; being a world champion and world record holder should help but it doesn't quite work like that.

Having Lizzie here with me is a huge boost. We mess around in the call room before the race, our tomfoolery only serving to make the other finalists all the more nervous. We have fun with it and walk out to our lanes ready for business. I'm in my element: we're outdoors, as we were in Rome, and there's a warmth in the light of a summer evening sky that reminds me how much I enjoy doing this. The deepth of light reminds me of the warmth and security I feel when I think of Mum.

At the half-way turn of the two-length race, I sense that I'm in the fight but have no idea where anyone else is. Later, the splits will show me that I turn third, more than half a second down on Daniela Samulski, from Germany. She's a pure sprinter and will struggle on the way back to the end wall. Lizzie turns second, just 0.03sec ahead of me. We're neck and neck and it's like that for much of the way home but I have always had a really strong last 50m and today is no different.

I look up. It's over. The scoreboard has a "1" by my name: my first European title is won in 59.80 seconds and Lizzie delivers another 1-2 for Britain in 1min 00.19, over half a second clear of the bronze won by Germany's other finalist, Jenny Mensing. I didn't have the opening speed I'm capable of when fully rested but I'm pleased that the back-end of my race reflects the work I've been putting in.

The last time Britain placed a woman on the 100m backstroke podium at the continental showcase was back in 1966. There's relief in knowing that I've lived up to expectation - my own and that of others - as a world champion. It's another great day for the British team. It shows that we're all in fine shape for the Commonwealth Games, our main aim this year.

On the seventh and last day of the championships, there's a twist in the tale of further success. In the medley relay, I give the girls a lead over Russia's Maria Gromova on backstroke, before Kate Haywood has to face European breast-stroke champion and Olympic medallist Yulia Efimova. Efimova gets a lightning start and has caught up in no time. Then it's over to Fran Halsall on butterfly, the chase on as Irina Bespalova fights hard to maintain Russia's lead. The picture is barely changed as Amy Smith tries to catch Margarita Nesterova on freestyle.

We're screaming our heads off as Amy inches closer and closer. The clock stops - 0.3sec shy for us. Russia have won. At major championships, the result is only confirmed when the scoreboard rolls and the results for each lane fall into their chronological finishing order, the winner on top. We're resigned to silver as we stand waiting for confirmation but several minutes after the last team comes home, the scoreboard remains unchanged.

Suddenly, the verdict flashes up: "1" - 3:59.72 Great Britain. Russia is down at the bottom of the heap with the letters DQ beside it. It turns out that Efimova leapt too soon, her eagerness resulting in disqualification for her team. The gold belongs to Britain for a third successive European Championship in this event. There's disappointment that we didn't take the title in our own right and deflation for the Russian girls. Even so, gold, no matter how it comes, is the best way you can end a meet.

This moment will mark the end of a time of winning for me, an end to feeling that I am fully fit in the context of world-class swimming. I've lived through a couple of years and more of being at the heart of things, in the mix, contributing to the lives of others, feeling as though I'm part of something much bigger than me, than swimming.

The Britain and England race schedule and a looming need to apply for a Green Card to stay in the United States contribute to the space that seems to be growing between my college years, my connection to the Gators squad and my life in Gainesville.

By the time I get back to Florida, I feel like I'm treading water out in the middle of a lake. I'm no longer a part of the things that have occupied my time and demanded my energy and focus. It is the start of a downward spiral. I've found nothing deeper to replace what is slipping away. I am struggling with what's becoming clear: I don't know which path to take next or even where I will be when I can no longer be at home in the States because I have no right to be there until I have a piece of paper that tells me I've been "approved".

My emotional roller-coaster has often been manageable because of the things I feel I'm able to control. I see a future in which things are about to be decided for me - and I don't like it.

CHAPTER 26

Thank You India

"Judge your success by what you had to give up in order to get it"

– DALAI LAMA XVI

The major championship of the summer traditionally ends sometime in early August and marks the moment when swimmers and coaches can take a breather before the start of a new cycle. This year is different: we're off to Delhi in October for the Commonwealth Games.

It's been a long haul from my final college season to the European Championships and now to India for England and what is supposed to be the highlight of the whole year, the culmination of hard work, the showcase result.

We've heard a lot of things about what it will be like in Delhi, how bad the Athletes' Village is, things falling behind schedule, venues not being ready. When we finally arrive from our luxury five-star camp in Doha fearing the worst, we're pleasantly surprised to see how normal it all looks. Ok, so the bed is not the most comfortable I've ever slept in but it will do. It is all new and it shows what they can provide.

I feel relaxed about it and I love being back on the national team. We're all having a lot of fun and there are a lot of youngsters I've never met before, with three places allowed for each home nation at Commonwealths, as opposed to the traditional two for the whole of Britain at other events such as the Olympics or world championships.

Joanne Jackson is a teammate who has won medals at all those levels. She's my roommate and the two of us are enjoying some really profound conversations. A couple of them go on long into the night. Fran Halsall and Lizzie Simmonds are across the hall in our apartment and there's a buzz between us all. I feel part of a family while away from my other family in America and my own blood family back in England. I feel I belong. I'm accepted. I've come such a long way from the girl I was before Beijing.

The team is full of tales of the animals that suddenly appear right before us on the pavement and in the middle of the road: monkeys, cows and even elephants. It's an amazing place, the sights, sounds and smells unlike anything I've experienced before. As we make our way from dorms to pool, we're fascinated by the bikes and mopeds that drone along the highways at a pace that reflects their load: to the right there's one with a huge cage full of chickens on the back; to the left a whole family, Mum, Dad and three kids, clinging to a tiny two-wheeler pumping it's way through fume and noise pollution.

It feels like I'm part of a camera crew on a movie set. A kaleidoscope of colour and cultures floats by as a hired-hand of a security man with a gun right in front of my face keeps us a safe distance from the thronging masses, a chaos of humanity and all its squalor and challenge. Two small children sit on the side of the road under a flimsy tarpaulin propped up by a stick or two; one is screaming at the top of his lungs, tears streaming down his face; the other stares impassively at us as we cruise by in our luxury bus. Heaven knows what that child is thinking.

The image haunts me at night as I drift into sleep. I wonder if I can harness the emotion of it to motivate me at a time when I'm struggling to keep the aquatic flame alive. Can I use it like I used my mother's fight against cancer? It's a disturbing thought. I fall asleep with images of dust clouds whirling behind our team bus and the police escorts we get to and from the pool. What are we doing here in a place where men with guns and dogs keep an uneasy world at bay and where there are more men and women to a job than I've ever seen before? What is this life about? How can people live in these conditions and how can I try to pick myself up to race when the very thought seems so trivial in the context of India?

I feel so very lucky to live the life I lead: to witness all these people in poverty; to see a baby alone and crying in pain or hunger or both by the side of the road; to catch a glimpse of a family living in a tent pegged to the kerb inches from potential disaster at the edge of the loudest, busiest highway I've ever seen. All of it pulls at my heartstrings. Thank you India. Thank you for making me realise just how lucky I am. Thank you providence. I am so incredibly blessed to have what I have, do what I do, be who I am, blessed to have the life I live.

At the pool, it feels like we've stepped back in time: this isn't what modern race pools are like. It is as though no-one let them know what was needed. I'm feeling fantastic in the water some days but awful on other days. That's what you expect in taper (when you rest in readiness to race in peak form).

There's a lot about the venue that is unexpected. The whole atmosphere is wrong: the water tastes differently to what we know modern pools to taste like; the place smells differently to what we're accustomed to, uncomfortably so; it doesn't feel clean; the venue is not race ready; this is not your standard competition pool. At some stage the toilets will overflow. It's just not what we're used to.

I've been conditioned to cope. That is what life in American swimming does for you if you let it. I figure that neither I nor the place are ready for racing but come race day, even if the pool leaves a lot to be desired, I will be ready because that is what I've trained to be. There's a lot of mind games being played, some allowing the conditions to throw them off course, others not. It shouldn't be this way but it is and you either get over it and step up or face the drop.

Coaches Troy and Wilby are back in Florida, where the pools are fit to race in. I talk to them on the phone about local conditions. Troy listens to what I have to say and tells me: remember, you are a step ahead of the game because others don't have the same coping mechanism that you have. Use that.

It seems that my past is actually helping me now, I know I've been through grief and the coaches know how to tap into that without making it a big deal. They let me know that I'm strong and that works for me because I've been through what I've been through and believe and know that I can cope. Other people struggle with the notion of recognising your strength as an aid to finding further strength. They don't believe in their own power, they have no coping mechanism and they can't figure it out until it's too late. The strength within each individual has to be owned by them, the strength within each individual is unique and powerful. Sometimes it deserts you.

First up, I have the 100m backstroke: my first big race since gold at the European Championships and I feel dreadful in morning heats. I don't feel the same drive I had, my motivation is weak and it shows: team staff sit me down and tell me that I don't look like me in the water and I'm not swimming the way Gemma Spofforth swims.

Not once on this trip have I really felt the kind of gut-wrenching sickness of good nerves that I felt at the world championships last year. I don't know how to create it either. In Rome last year I was willing to spend the day with butterflies rippling through my stomach until all the nervousness in me was gone. Not here: I feel no nervousness. I feel flat. I don't have the hunger I once had nor the will to race back-to-back finals. Have I let the conditions affect me or am I suffering burnout? Do I really want it - any of it - any more?

Usually, come the big occasion, speed is natural. Here, I'm having to really focus on swimming fast, double my concentration and make deliberate efforts to ignore all the distractions around me, including all the chat about conditions that are hard to ignore.

I sit in the call room before the final and hear the other girls saying how hard it is to see the flags that serve as markers to warn you that you're 5m from the wall. I think "no it's not. I've seen every flag so far, no trouble". I go out and have a really good opening 50, turn well and know that my last length is better than anyone else's in the race. Then, I get my first taste of poor environment: I can't see the flags going into the end wall and, having missed them altogether, I end up finishing the race with my head on the wall, the time lost equivalent to an outstretched arm. In sprint swimming, that's an ocean.

Emily Seebohm, of Australia, gets to the wall first, in 59.79. The time is just 0.01sec faster than that in which I won the European title back in the summer. By now, I was supposed to have been faster, Delhi the priority for this season. I stop the clock at 1:00.02 for silver. I hate coming second. Even though it was not a bad swim, considering my mental strength and waning motivation right now, silver is small consolation for not getting what I came for. I came to win. My finish cost me gold.

Sport is about what happens, not what might have been and by the time I leave the pool deck I'm angry and want to make good. I recall how I felt when I took bronze in the 100m backstroke at the European juniors championships back in 2004; I came back the next day and channelled my emotions into a gold-medal-winning performance over 200m.

Here in Delhi the day after silver, raw emotion guides me to the water for the 50m backstroke heats and I set a Commonwealth Games record. The semi goes well too but the final falls in the same session as the 200m final, a bizarre programming error by organisers. I finish fifth in the 200m as Lizzie gets touched out for gold by Aussie Meagan Nay by just 0.33sec. To add insult to injury, an hour later I'm back in to face a fresh Australian, Sophie Edington, who sneaks gold in the 50m just 0.03sec ahead of me.

I'm fuming. It's pieces of silver for a third time on the last day of racing, when I join England teammates Kate Haywood, Ellen Gandy and Fran Halsall in the 4x100m medley relay. The Australians take gold and Seebohm sets a Games record of 59.53 in the lead-off 100m backstroke leg. I come home in 59.83. It's second all the way through the meet.

I'm frustrated. It has been a hellishly long season and it feels like it. I call Wilby. He's disappointed in the situation, whereas I'm disappointed in me. I'd planned to be at my best this year here in India. It hasn't worked out like that and only sometime later, when I'm looking at photos comparing what physical shape I was in for Rome in 2009 and then Delhi, will I realise that my expectations might have been too optimistic: I'm not in the same place at all. As for my mental strength, there's no comparison.

I'm not sure if there was a specific moment this year when I set off on a downward spiral but Delhi has highlighted my predicament. Coming out of big meets, successful or not, I've always had something to turn to: the next college season, school; crisis intervention; another focus. Now, it feels like I have nothing.

I've thrived on being a part of something much bigger than me. It's an amazing feeling to be out on the water, to be out in the middle of a lake: you can float there and know that you are somehow insignificant yet part of a cosmic world of beauty and enjoy being just that. My time in Florida has been like that: at the centre of things but a cog in the wheel, a cog helping other cogs and eventually a chief cog but never in the limelight.

Leadership in swimming is about following the people we're leading by empowering them to take responsibility for what they do. My college days are over and I have nothing like that to look forward to after Delhi. I feel lost with nowhere to go. I feel vulnerable and exposed, as though it is all about me and no longer where I fit in the network of people making this journey with me. My lake has run dry. I feel less significant. I'm no longer part of a whole. I'm just me, stranded on a boat with no water to float on.

My emotions are raw as I wait for a flight back to Europe. I regret not having made the most of the week. The costly poor finish in the 100m is still stinging. I wanted gold. It could have been gold, should have been gold. I think a lot about everything on the way home. I will spend a little time in

Britain and Italy on the way back to Gainesville. It should be exciting but I'm even finding the travelling monotonous.

I'm questioning everything. Am I even excited to go back to America? I know there's no other place for me yet I'm anxious about returning this time. I feel confused about where I should be for the first time since deciding to be in Florida. My Britain teammate Jemma Lowe has left, returned home to Wales. That sets me to thinking whether I too would be better off back home, where I might get better recognition and even funding.

Yet still I'm drawn back to the team and life I love in Gainesville. The sun, the coaches, my family at the crisis center are all things I yearn for. The more I think about it, the more I feel that my anxiety is all about the college team environment and season that I'm no longer eligible to be a part of. It feels like I'm being forced to wave goodbye to a dear friend.

India and the results in the pool there have stirred up a psychological storm in me. There's so much I need to work on, so many questions to answer: how to ease my mind of the pressure I feel yet fill it with the edge of nervousness needed to win; how to understand what it is to be mentally tough; how to practise not preach; how to hate coming second but know how to harness that and do something about it. Will I be able to use my Delhi deliverance as fodder for the next two years or is this turmoil going to send me off course?

My mood and load is lightened by a fabulous day in Milan with the Italian people from the suitmaker Jaked and two days of relaxation and a lovely lunch with my Dad and brother. It was only then that Delhi belly hit me properly: I'd escaped the worst of what laid low so many on the team back in India. At least now I have a clean loo to pop to when nature calls.All too soon, I'm back at another airport and finally heading home to Gainesville, though not for long. I have a temporary visa until Christmas and then I will have to leave and live outside the States until my application for a Green Card, which allows non-Americans to live and work in the US, is approved. It will take months. I feel like a puppet on someone else's string.

Up above the clouds over the Atlantic, my mind drifts back to India: the patrols, the guard dogs and even guard monkeys, the barbed wire around the Athletes' Village; the squalor, colour, sounds and smells. If I felt safe, I also felt uncomfortable. Had I been dealt a different hand by life, I might have been there, living in that filth and firestorm. A pang of guilt runs through me as I recall what it felt like to gaze out at the other side of life from the bubble of a bus full of privileged, well-cared-for athletes, celebrities and sufferers divided by a sheet of glass and the threat of force.

The results in the pool pale by comparison to an experience that barely grazed the surface of India but felt like a skydive into an alien world, one in which I felt helpless. It stirs in me the very forces that pointed me towards counselling and working with underprivileged kids. There are people who need my help and it's good to know that I don't have to sit there watching helplessly. I can get up and do something about it.

Thank you India.

CHAPTER 27

Green Card, Christmas with Liz and Matt

"It's so hard to forget pain, but it's even harder to remember sweetness. We have no scar to show for happiness. We learn so little from peace"

— CHUCK PALAHNIUK

I can't recall a more unsettling time since Mum died. I feel disconnected from the Gators, the college, the life that was in Gainesville and now I have to leave Florida while awaiting approval of my Green Card application. As if to make matters worse, I'm heading back to England and a home that has been visited by cancer once more. The parallels with the past, including seeking solace in swimming, are painful.

My plan is to spend Christmas at home and then base myself at Loughborough University's Intensive Training Centre in early 2011 with coach Kevin Renshaw. That's a deliberate move: Lizzie Simmonds is part of the squad there, under the guidance of coach Ben Titley. While we will often be in the same pool, we won't be working side by side every day. There'll be no "Britain's top two backstroke swimmers in daily battle!"

Apart from overseas camps, I am in Britain now until after the World Championship trials in April. I miss my friends in Gainesville but the break will help me to change my perspective on things: it will get me away from the monotony of what I've been doing, allow me to try something else and, I hope, get back my love of swimming. I'm heading out of my comfort zone: a new coach, a new training base, a new stimulus and a change in scenery.

I'm no longer in school but I will read more books in the next three months than I've read in my whole life. I need the distraction.

We've been thrown a ticking bomb with no clock to tell us how long before the detonation. I struggle to fathom how my Dad and my brother are able to show so much strength as events unfold. June White, Dad's girlfriend of three years, has terminal cancer. It is four years since the death of his wife, my Mum. June attends the same places that Mum had to visit when she was ill and she is cared for in the same hospice, St Wilfrid's in Chichester, in which Mum passed away. As if there had not been enough sorrow, June's daughter Vicky has also diagnosed with cancer.

On the way to Britain, it helps to have my fellow Gator, Matt, travelling with me. He's been a friend for a long time. There have been times when he's been a great comfort. Even though his ability to talk until the cows come home is a welcome distraction from thoughts of what I'll find when I arrive home, I'm ready to punch him in the face by the time his visit is done: it may be the only thing that will stop him from talking!

Matt's not the only yuletide visitor: Liz Goldson and her entire family are over from the States to remind us of the great Christmas we had at their place in New York two years ago. Everyone's getting on really well. We find time to get to London and explore the capital and we take in an Arsenal match because Liz's brother is a big fan. I'm not a big follower of football but I enjoy the moment in good company.

Besides, it's good to escape the house for a little while. Disease - because that is what it feels like - and looming dread underpin the genuine happiness and gratitude we all feel for having had the chance to be together this Christmas under one roof. Where there's laughter, there's also the sound of Vicky having to blow her nose a lot because of her condition; pills are being taken on a regular basis. It gnaws at us.

Despite it all, Dad is handling things remarkably well. He's doing a good job of being the man of the house - and a Grandad figure too: there are three young children in the house, Vicky's son and her sister's two children.

I'm worried that Dad is not letting his feelings show, is not able to express himself and talk about things. When I'm sad and I know I'm with people who can take it, I find talking helps a lot. I think Dad would benefit from doing that but it doesn't work like that for him. Maybe it doesn't work like that for most men.

Peter has been there for Dad a lot more often than I've been. My brother works in London in a bank, in mergers and acquisitions. I'm so proud of him. He's just 21 but he's helping to advise multi-billion dollar companies. Where I've been at least eight hours away by plane, he's a couple of hours from home. June's condition reminds me of the guilt I felt because I wasn't there to help Mum go through what she went through. I didn't want it all to fall on Dad and Peter.

At times like these, it is so important, though not at all easy, to live for the moment. That is what this Christmas has been about: family, mine, my extended one, and the importance of these people to me. I let that thought be my guide until it's time to leave for Loughborough and one of the toughest parts of this journey I'm on.

Ahead of me lies a new challenge, a fresh environment, a training camp in Australia. I have so much to look forward to and yet, at the same time, I feel as though circumstances are preventing me from moving on.

There's been talk of June going into a hospice. It would be the same place where I last held my Mum's hand and took the Christmas present back from her when she had no energy left to open it. The memory breaks my heart.

What is happening now is anchoring me to the past. History repeats itself at home in England and a part of my life in Gainesville that has caused me heartache travels with me Down Under and takes me deep into the well.

CHAPTER 28

Down (But Not Out) Down Under

"There are so many fragile things, after all. People break so easily and so do dreams and hearts"

— NEIL GAIMAN

Up on the angel's shoulder 23 floors high in an apartment block that looks out over the Pacific Ocean, the views are to die for. Literally, this night.

The Australian Gold Coast stretches out as far as the eye can see either side of my temporary home in a training camp with British teammates. The sound of spilling waves from the shoreline way down below floats up on southern summer night air. Ironic. Like the rhythm of water and wind, my will to live this life ebbs and flows.

One moment the seascape is there, the next it is gone, lost in the dark well into which I'm descending. Nature's gifts and those I have been blessed with are blocked by an overriding thought: is the ground all those 23 storeys down hard enough - and would it be a very good thing to hit?

It doesn't matter that the waves roll, that the water is there for me to dive into. The thought going through my mind is how solid the ground might be and whether it would be enough to take me from this world. The balcony is so high: I could jump right now and then I wouldn't have to 'deal with it', wouldn't have to have all the stress. I am arguing with myself again, thinking 'no you can't do that'.

The nature of concrete competes for attention with the glorious nature fading in and out around me. The ocean, the warm air, the lights and humming of cars way down below are not always there but they come back enough to show me that the world is there and that I can still be on this planet and feel it. At the deepest place in the well, I'm here but not here.

I'm three weeks into the camp with Loughborough coach Kevin Renshaw, his team and coach Dave McNulty's squad from Bath's Intensive Training Centre. We're preparing for the World Championship trials back in Britain that will, hopefully, provide the ticket to the defence of my title from Rome in 2009. I'm here because I need to be somewhere while waiting for my US Green Card to come through so that I can return home to Florida.

Kevin's been great when it comes to adult conversation about what I'm going through. He doesn't delve too deeply into emotions. I say 'this and that's happening, this is what I feel and watch out for it because if I break down you'll know why'. He gets it.

I did the same with Wilby back in Florida when Mum was living with cancer. I would tell him what was happening so that if I broke down in a training set, he kind of knew that it wasn't because I wasn't getting on with someone but because of what was going on back home. Now, it feels like I'm living the nightmare all over again: June, my Dad's new partner, has been diagnosed with cancer, the dreaded disease that ruins lives and rips through families like a hurricane.

I can see her in my mind's eye: not too long after we'd first met, June loading the dishwasher at our family home, turning to me, smiling. I treasure the open communication she instigated.

The phone calls back home leave me feeling miserable. They're not doing well. I think about Mum all the time. Everything floods back, including that painful understanding that I wasn't there for Mum and Dad back then and now I'm not there for Dad and June. How am I supposed to feel this time? June is not someone I should love, not someone I am really involved with. I'm desperately worried about Dad . but to be honest, I'm feeling as sorry for myself.

An amazing life on the one hand, guilt on the other. I feel so low, so conflicted: I love my life, love being in Australia but from home comes a reminder that maybe I shouldn't.

We've had three weeks of an amazing camp. It's been a breeze with Jo Jackson, Roberto Pavoni and others and it has all come at a good time for me: I've been wondering whether I really want to keep swimming. The great company, the sunbathing and experiencing life up until this night on the balcony has been really good for me but even though I consider these people to be friends of mine I don't feel able to burden them with what's going through my head.

I know I could speak to Jo, our bond sealed through our experiences in India at the Commonwealth Games. Here in Australia, Jo is in our apartment but in a separate bedroom with Jess Dickons. They're sleeping and I don't want to wake them. I'm rooming with my Gator teammate Stephanie Proud. She's also asleep. Besides, she is not someone to whom I relate well. I've been very passive aggressive towards her. I don't tell Steph what I need to say or what I mean to say. I don't ever get across what I should have got across on many occasions. I can't speak to her about June, my Dad, my feelings. She's just wired differently: we both speak English but it seems we speak different languages. There is so much about her that I admire, yet I find it so difficult to communicate my emotions to her.

We've lived together for five years in Florida and that's why we're put in a room together on camps and teams. The truth is, Steph is not someone I can turn to. I do not in any way blame her for my state of being as I sit here on the balcony but I also feel that I cannot communicate my emotions to her. I feel trapped. I am paralysed by searing emotions, unable to think about who to call, where to turn to.

It has taken five years or more to even manage to communicate in language splintered by awkwardness. Before Steph moved out to Florida I had already known that our friendship might be strained. When we were younger, we never truly clicked and she was always the person who was faster, the junior who was going to be big, a swimmer everyone looked up to. I'd even told coach Wilby before she arrived: "... fine that she comes but I can't tell you that we'll be friends".

Understandably, he was confused when I then told him that she was going to move in with me and that I'd helped her get a scooter, helped move her stuff from the dorms because her parents weren't there. I went above and beyond to try to help her out.

You may well ask why. Why would I walk into what was surely going to be a challenging situation? Call it a learning curve. I was already living with two other people. Steph came out to Florida late and we'd all settled in, we all had friends, we all had cliques. She was walking home to dinner with me one day and saying "it really worries me that I'm not going to find someone to room with". It was at that point that I found my heart softening. I asked: "So why not move in with us?" We got on a little better and a friendship of sorts started to develop.

Back then, before the lessons I've learnt, I tried very hard to figure out how to like people I didn't like. Tried to work out how to make my life easier and have a relationship with people I didn't get on with, find a path that avoided me having to simply ignore them. With Steph, barriers of language, personality and outlook make for a rocky friendship. I struggle with it and try to force myself to fix us.

Bring me adversity and challenge and I will embrace it - but not alone, as such. There is a dual, or even multiple, personality in me: one side wants to get through it and will fight for it, the other side says "I give up - I don't want to deal with it!"

That sums up my struggle here on the balcony this night. I'm inviting darkness into the room. It's a form of self-harm, a way of trying to figure out how to be strong when I have something that I might potentially harm myself with. I need something to help me build myself up. It would be great to carry to the London 2012 Olympics what I felt in Rome but how to harness the thing that wounds so you can get the best out of yourself in another area of life?

I've approached a couple of races like that. At trials in Scotland before Rome back in 2009, I was rooming with Steph. I was getting so angry with her over misunderstandings we had. My anger came across in the 200m: I was fuming all the way to the pool, the rage building gradually in me. I harnessed it in the race and set a British record of 2mins 07.56. That and a 2:08.81 season best from Lizzie Simmonds set us both up for a fantastic year.

Channelling anger into the water was my way of dealing with difficulty and using the different personalities in me to best effect in the water. I compartmentalise myself a lot. I could not have taken that anger and used it on dry land with Steph. When I'm in the pool, it's swimming, and when I'm out of the pool its counsellor Gemma or dog-owner Gemma or any other Gemma I may be. There are all sorts of parts to me that make up the whole. It is almost as if I do have all these different personalities and they argue with each other.

That character has grown out of circumstance and need. I don't remember being like this before Mum's death. Events have left me much more in tune with my emotions. Here on the balcony, I'm angry and frustrated but I recognise such feelings for what they are and how you can work with them because of my training at the crisis center.

I counsel myself: Gemma the counsellor counsels Gemma the swimmer. One thinks "jump", the other rationalises. A crowd of neurons start a food fight with each other in my head. Each of them says "my turn to fight now". My brain juggles with multiple choice.

The biggest thing for me, as thoughts flow of a concrete end to understanding my grief, is that I am a suicide counsellor. I tell myself "'there's no way you can even think about jumping right now because that would make you the biggest hypocrite in the world. How many times have you sat with others in this moment?"

I listen to the questions and the answers in me. I listen to me. That's one thing we are taught to do as counsellors, to actively listen to the person going through it. It is harder to do that when you are the only person there. I tell myself "you have the right to be angry, you have the right to be sad, the right to be angry with other people".

Had I not been there before, not had the training, things might have worked out differently but suicide, a scary thought for most, is not a taboo for me. It is a part of my life and it's ok for me to think about it and ok for me to think my way out of it. Standing here on the balcony there are moments when all thought is clouded. I'm at the bottom of a well, there's nothing, no means to help me get out. I'm in pitch darkness, with no means of escape.

As a counsellor I talk about everything that a person is feeling, tell them to stay in that well, get in the well with them, keep them in as much darkness as I can. That way, you let them know that it's ok to feel like that, that what they feel is valid because of x, y and z. I even delve deeper into the well if needs be. In that sense, I am not scared by what is happening.

I stay in the well until I've processed my thoughts and feelings. The next thing is to work out what the future is. There is no rope here, no way out. I feel turmoil, my mind tumbling through thought after thought about how it is ok to think like this, ok to say 'This is the place where it is ok to say 'enough'.

I talk my way around it, through it, down from it and back into the apartment. There's ice-cream in the freezer. I eat a pint of ice-cream, eating through my emotions as I go. I end up sleeping on the couch for two or three hours. We are leaving for Britain the next day and I rationalise it simply enough: staying up late was just a way of starting to live in the home time zone again.

I greet the dawn. My new teammates are there. Business as usual. The journey home is a blur but when we get back to Britain, I drive up to Loughborough, Steph with me, and we drop teammate Daniel Fogg off before going to the dorms where we'll be staying before the World Championship trials in Manchester.

It is uncomfortable but I feel fine: I'm still alive; still swimming; still living life as the pale, March sun shines through trees; the British countryside

Dealing With It

is about to awaken in another season of green, another new beginning; I'm still working towards my goals; my Dad is still proud of me; my brother still calls me all the time. Those feelings are the fuel that keeps the engine running.

CHAPTER 29

Troubles Shared; Troubles Halved

"One of the most beautiful qualities of true friendship is to understand and to be understood"

– LUCIUS ANNAEUS SENECA

The family home is full of the past, the signs of cancer everywhere I look. There's a disabled seat on the toilet to help June, bottles of pills line surfaces and alarms go off to remind her when to take her medicine. She's pale and drawn, her face and body reflecting the pain she's in. Just like Mum did, June is staying strong: she's getting on with life as best she can.

To see her like this not only tells me a lot about what she's going through but reminds me that it must have been like this for my own Mum at a time when I was not here to help, not here to witness it, not here to hold her hand. The thought bites at me.

The circumstances would have been the same - only I wasn't there. Mostly, my Mum was a voice at the other end of the line, sometimes crying but always adamant that she wanted me to get on with my life and live our dream of swimming and college in the US. Now I'm here, seeing it with my own eyes and I wonder how much time I missed with Mum, time that would have been so precious, time we will never get back. I escape for a while when the first boy I ever knew intimately, Philip, calls and asks if we can have a drink together. He's just out of the Army and he talks about his aspirations, his feelings and the life he'd like to lead.

It takes my mind off things for a short while but distraction doesn't last. When I get home, I need to tell someone how I'm feeling before I slump so far down that I'll never get up.

I send an email to my housemate, friend and fellow crisis counsellor, David Marra.

Gemma:

Sorry this mail is so long. Miserable :(

I don't know why it is so much easier to make everyone spill their guts to me than it is for me to ask someone to listen but I am really struggling today. I've resorted to writing because every time I even start to think about talking to someone about it my throat closes up and I find the water in my eyes welling to the point of escalation, where I can't imagine stopping crying even with the best crisis center folks on the other end!!

I even have tears in my eyes now and feel this might be better for me! Anyhow, I don't want to pile all this shit on you but I do want to get it in writing and off my shoulders a little... I know you won't mind and for that I feel a little guilty!! ha-ha - why am I such a hypocrite?!?

Anyways, I came home home for the weekend to spend time with my family and I am really struggling to stay strong or even try and communicate even my smallest feelings with them about everything that is going on...

My Dad's girlfriend is deteriorating majorly in health, in and out of the hospice that my Mum was in and out of, seeing the size of her feet because she can't move off the couch easily and seeing the toilet I grew up in as a disabled one and seeing all the pills makes me wonder how much of this I missed when Dad and my brother went through it with my Mum, makes me wonder how many times my Mum referenced suicide like June does multiple times a day because the pain in her back is too much to bear, how many doctors came and went like they are now.

So this wouldn't be too bad for me to bear, maybe, if June's daughter wasn't just diagnosed with inoperable cancer again for the 4th time now and is having to go through chemo again and then Vicky's (June's daughter) son has a pain in his back too, which they are checking on soon!

Well, I guess what I am most upset about is all the pain that I feel from seeing Dad go through all this and not communicate, just "soldier on", as by brother puts it. Like he goes to work and then goes to see his Mum, who doesn't remember who he is much or whether she is on holiday or who has moved her clothes, as she has recently gone into a home, then he comes home to literally waiting hand and foot on anything June needs because her quality of life is so bad at the moment that she literally needed me in the kitchen while she tried to peel potatoes because she wanted to feel like she could do something.

I came home to try and support but all I know is emotional support I don't know anything else and I feel like I am the least emotionally stable out of all of us. Of course, I do anything and everything I can to help, help cook, etc., but it's not enough; I know he is coping, but is that enough, is it enough to cope in a situation like this? And I don't even know what I am expecting, like, do I want him just to completely crack and go into emotional crisis because that's what I feel like I am doing and it's all because I am empathizing with him?

Anyways, I'm sorry for my epic email I just felt like I needed to share it.

The next day, February 21, 2011, the exchange flows:

David:

Firstly, I want to thank you A) for trusting me and telling me all of this and for FINALLY OPENING UP! I know you always have to be the rock for everyone to lean on and that isn't easy! I've told you I'm always here for you and I'm so honored that you finally opened up to me.

As for everything else, I can't even imagine what you are going through. You're world must be crashing down around you. Everywhere you look you see physical pain and emotional suffering with the people you love.

Seeing your Dad in so much pain is unbearable. You know how much he is suffering but he wont let anyone in on it. It's tearing him up inside and thus tearing you up inside. You hate to see him go through this again.

Being home is bringing back such painful memories for you of your mom. As painful as it is to see someone your Dad cares about suffer, it's killing you because you are struggling with painful memories and guilt. It sounds like you feel guilty because you weren't there for your mom when she was dying like your brother and your Dad were. Even though your mom told you to stay in the US you probably feel like you had an obligation to be here with your mom and suffer with her as she was dying.

You are always the person people lean on but if a cornerstone is crumbling from the weight of an edifice, what supports the cornerstone from crumbling? You feel like you have to be strong for your Dad and your brother but it's killing you.

You're a wreck and you needed someone to be there for YOU. And I'm glad that it was me who gets to be there for you.

Gemma:

Thanks love, you are completely correct with everything, hit the nail on the head. June is back in the hospice again this week and they are trying to put an epidural in for the pain. It's strange because every time I think about that and Dad's pain, it's ok, until I feel all the emotions I must have suppressed or not processed properly from Mum. I know nothing can change and I know that life goes on in the face of a crisis or after the fact it's just really hard. And it is so much easier to put it down in words than it is to talk openly about it. Thank you for being there I appreciate it more than you know.

David:

You said that you never allowed yourself to properly suffer for your mom. You just used all that anger/frustration/agony, and put it towards swimming. You were able to do this probably because you never had to see your mom on a daily basis. It was easier to put up a front and be strong and "soldier on".

Now that seeing this suffering is becoming a daily routine and it's inescapable, it seems reasonable that all the emotions you pushed aside from your mom are coming flooding back.

On top of the normal emotions you probably felt, I'm sure you are dealing with a lot of guilt too. Guilt that you never suffered to the extent that your Dad or your brother did. That you never had to deal with this pain everyesay. To look into the face of someone who knows they are going to die and watch them wither away.

For you, it's probably like watching your mom die all over again. And that is agonizing.

Gemma:

Yea - but I am not seeing it on a daily routine, just on the weekend that I went home. And then I feel guilty again for not being there for Dad again. I feel like I can't win, like I know that they won't let me be there, and that I'll even will get in the way if I am, but then that makes me feel useless and, yes, I do feel guilty for not being there but I'm constantly arguing that with myself because she didn't (they didn't) want me there. And I feel like if I am only half witnessing this, then I must have barely witnessed my Mum's pain and so: what and how does my Dad cope?!David:

And I'm sure feeling useless is something that's totally foreign to you. It sounds like you are fighting a losing battle and feel defeated. How can you help if they won't let you?

Gemma:

Damn - you are good at this! That's exactly how I feel!

Some of the time I feel like I am gaining strength and working it out, I know that time heals and everything but it's not a very quick process and I am loosing the fight and anger in swimming and trying to process and therefore losing the power that made me swim fast in the 1st place, what if I can't ever get to where I was because I am processing ... I'm healthier mentally and emotionally because of it but am I failing in my profession because of it too! And therefore failing the legacy that my Mum left behind - and I'm not one of those who says 'I only swim for Mum' and I do know she would be proud of me no matter what but there are so many people who count on me to swim fast or show strength and continue to do that; when I start to imagine that, maybe the pressure is getting too much - and it's almost time for London 2012 and people are expecting things ... what if I fail?

David:

That's so difficult. What made you a great swimmer is this pent up anger and frustration but it's slowly killing you inside. It's either your health or success in the pool. Perhaps since your mom told you to stay in school and not come back to England when she was dying that you feel like YOU HAVE to win and you have to succeed otherwise you will be failing your mom.

And then you have not only the weight of your mom's memory but the weight of a NATION coming up in 2012. You have to do great otherwise it's not only failing your mom's legacy, which you always said you swam for but failing England. To win makes you a national hero and an icon and will memorialize your mom forever, but to fail is to be a disappointment to millions of people. Geeze, how do you not crack under the pressure?

I know that I can't even imagine what you are going through and to even try to understand is futile, therefore advice or my opinion would be useless. However, you said so yourself, you are a swimmer, but that isn't who you are. What you are is an amazing counselor, a wonderful daughter, a great sister, an amazing friend, and then an athlete. Whether you get first place or last in any race, you've already succeeded a major part of your life because you've overcome adversity and you've touched the lives of some many people.

Dealing With It

The next day, I reply:

All I can really say after that one is: you just put a really big smile on my face!! Again, I appreciate you more than you can ever know and thank you so much for being so perfect that I can trust you with this.

CHAPTER 30

June White Dies

"Things, well, things suck sometimes. Sometimes you can fix it and sometimes you can't. It's just the way it is"

— ELIZABETH SCOTT

With David's words of wisdom buoying my spirits, I head to Manchester for Britain's world-championship trials. It's early March 2011 and the mournful grey sky overhead reminds me how far away we are from Australia, Florida and the outdoor summer season I so love. I'm not in the same place, neither mentally nor physically, as I was when I won the world 100m backstroke crown in Rome.

I'm constantly striving to find ways to motivate myself, to track down the competitive edge that went missing somewhere along the way, the stuffing seemingly knocked out of me by circumstance.

I try to harness my work at the crisis center by reminding myself every time I'm having a bad day that there are people out there with much bigger problems, people much worse off than myself. It helps me to work a little harder but what I'm looking for is something to make me race faster.

I think back to Delhi and the picture of poverty and dismay that haunts me yet. I know that the pain of Mum's death was also something that once drove me to new heights in the pool. But whatever I try now, I can't get back the hunger, the desire, the fight.

Before trials, I toy with the concept of creating fake emotions as a motivator. When I first think about it, I imagine I'm racing a shark. I could associate the inherent danger and malevolence with the competitor in the next lane. I lock eyes with the shark and focus on its big, sharp teeth as I get ready to race it.

Come the day in Manchester, I see no sharks in the pool. I haven't quite got my head around the concept of helpful imagery but at least my mention of sharks to a reporter has made a headline - and made me laugh.

I'm left to rely on the incentive of having a world title to defend and a British title to regain after Lizzie Simmonds beat me in the national championship 100m backstroke final a year ago. I race the heats and semi-finals of the 100m on the second day. I get a good night's rest and head into the final optimistic that I'll make the cut. No-one seems to be swimming that fast and in 1min 00.52sec, I win and book my ticket to the big event in Shanghai come July.

Lizzie Simmonds finishes second but her time misses the target. I'm extremely dissatisfied with my performance but my focus is on Lizzie: I empathize with her and I give her a huge hug as tears well in her eyes. My listening skills kick in. I just want to help her through this, she is such an amazing athlete, she's humorous, profound and great company too. We've spent many hours contemplating life and how to change the world, her wit and intellect on a par with her success in the pool. I wonder what it will be like without her Irish jigs, her larking about and laughter in the pre-race call room in China. I've got used to them and her being a part of my approach.

We spend a long time in the shower and she shares some of her private thoughts about where she is emotionally and why. We discuss fear, pain, disappointment, how to get back up for the next race. It's good to have such trust. I'm not sure there are many other rivalries that enjoy such a deeply ingrained friendship.

Two days later, I'm getting ready for the 200m. The day goes well, I have dinner with friends and head off to get some sleep. It's 10pm when I have a sudden urge to call Dad. I know straight away that something is wrong, his voice cracking under the strain of it all, I recognize the sound of his voice and feel the tight ball of constriction in my throat once more. June is unlikely to make it through the night, he tells me. This may well be the last night of her life and if it is she will die in the same place, St Wilfrid's Hospice in Chichester, where Mum spent her final hours before succumbing to the same illness.

The floor seems to fall away beneath me, I feel myself sliding, with nothing and no-one to stop me. Dad changes the subject and starts talking about swimming and how I'm doing. How he can do that is beyond me. I feel sick. Tears stream down my face as I try to keep my voice as level as possible. I answer some of his questions and then freeze, almost forgetting every single lesson I had been taught in crisis intervention: "do you want to talk about it"; "it's devastating and infuriating"; "how are you feeling"?

After a brief conversation I feel exhausted; I text a few people asking if they're awake and then crawl into the bed next to Steph Proud, my roommate once more. She gives me a hug. My phone rings and I leave the room to take a call from Wilby. He tries to help me to make sense of the pain I'm feeling, cope with a feeling of guilt that stems from this being about Dad and June, not about me.

Lowri Tynan, a Welsh breaststroke swimmer, comes out into the corridor and we stand by a window overlooking the ferris wheel outside the hotel. Her warm heart and beautiful personality settles me. She stays with me; we laugh and cry a lot and when we're done I finally crawl back into bed and fall asleep. It's 2am.

About five hours later, I awake to a text message from Dad: "She died peacefully ... at 2am". I want more than anything else in the world to leave Manchester and go home to Dad and comfort him but a second text tells me: "please stay and finish the job in Manchester". It would be a distraction for him to keep an eye on what I was doing, he says.

The heats of the 200m backstroke await. I arrive at the pool and walk once around the deck. I never do that. I'm confused, dazed. This swimming home I always feel so comfortable in, so much a part of, feels different today. I don't really know why I'm here, what I'm doing. Any sense of purpose has abandoned me. I can't focus on a single thing.

Steph qualifies for the final just ahead of Lizzie and me with a second to spare. My time is slow. It feels like I'm leaving things to chance. Later that day, Lizzie qualifies for the world championships, the rest of us miss out, the time target ahead of us. I finish fifth, well away from my best. I spend my time between the water and the media mixed zone where reporters await to interview us thinking of what to say. Wilby has been a towering strength on such occasions and has taught me to come up with "quote B" if "quote A" is something that is going to cause me to break down when I don't want to.

A smile etched on my face, I tell the journalists that it's been "a bad day at the office" and that it's been a tough time being away from the US awaiting my Green Card and unable to be home in Florida.

There was truth in that but the detail was too devastating and infuriating to explain. How could this happen to Dad, to us, again? Why June; why now? Guilt returns to kick me once more. There's light relief at lunch with Craig Lord, a reporter for The Times. I manage to tell him what's happened. We discuss my work on this book. I feel the process will not only help me but others too. I'm hopeful that that will be the case but by the time the championships are over, pessimism has settled on me like fog.

I hate it but I'm forced to face it: events are turning me into someone I didn't want to be. The ambivalence in me - I neither expected June to live nor to die - will soon be a thing of the past. Before the year is out, cancer will claim June's daughter Vicky too and the change in me will be complete: from now on, if I hear someone has cancer, I will assume they are going to die. The optimist in me has been drowned by experience.

You'd never know it by reading the papers or watching the TV coverage of the trials. My parting shot is delivered with a smile and a happy outlook: I have a six-month visa to take me back home to Gainesville and my Green Card will be activated sometime in the summer. Can't wait, a much needed escape from the drowning memories of cancer.

The trials done, I attend June's funeral. It's a bleak time, sorrow blanketing the first buds of spring. I feel as though a curse has befallen us.

CHAPTER 31

Shanghai Sorrow and Troy's Truth

"Failure is success if we learn from it"

— MALCOLM FORBES

When the official at the US embassy, as well as a few others along the way, asked me why I was so keen to return to Florida after the world-championships trials in Manchester, I told them: "I want to train out there, I have made a family out there, I have my work at the crisis center and I am not ready to leave yet."

All true - but I've been away for many months now and things have changed. I'm no longer a part of the college swimming group and there are some new faces in the pool, including swimmers who've turned "pro". I'm not quite sure where I fit. I feel a little lost. I'm delighted to be back in Gainesville but the world has shifted and everyone is deep into their own plans and aspirations for the year.

I go training but not with the intensity or purpose I've had in the past and by the time I have to turn round again and leave for the Britain camp in

Osaka, Japan, on the way to the world championships in Shanghai, I'm not sure what to expect.

It helps to return to somewhere familiar: arriving in Osaka again three years after our pre-Olympic camp before Beijing, I know instantly where we are and where to go and where to find things. It isn't the kind of cultural shock we felt back in 2008. I know where to get the train (and understand the station noises) and where to find the chocolate. Everything's very organised.

China is another matter: If you think Italy is a risky option on the roads, think ten times as bad and you have an idea of what Shanghai is like. This is a vast, buzzing, bumping, bellowing cosmopolitan city brimming with people on the move. On the one hand, at 6ft I'm much bigger than most of the people swarming around me; on the other I feel like an ant.

In Beijing during the Games we had time and opportunity to explore a little of the culture, to take in some sights. It felt otherworldly, a very different place from home. Here in Shanghai, we're ferried backwards and forwards to the pool, the distances are huge and there's no time to see anything other than the blur from behind the windows of the team bus. We're screened from the sounds and smells of the city, locked on the quiet side of the westernised bubble of Shanghai: the city looks far removed from many of the images of China we see and hear of on our screens and publications back home. Here is the more modern face of a land that remains remote from the rest of the world in many ways.

The swimming venue is on a colossal scale. Several pools, one singularly devoted to diving, stand one side of an artificial lake running down the middle of a complex built for China-sized crowds. On the other side of the water is a palatial convention-type building housing an International Swimming Hall of Fame exhibition of the sport's history.

Approaching race day, my head is not in the right place but that turns out to be the least of my worries. My championships are over before they begin. The night before the 100m backstroke heats, I'm sitting on the floor in the corridor outside my room with a trash can in which to catch the vomit. The little guard who keeps watch on our landing approaches me several times to ask if I need help. I keep telling him to go away because it's going to get nasty but he seems not to want to listen. I'm too sick to worry about it.

Finally, I give in and ask to see Ian Gordon, our team doctor. His care sees me through the night. Hope alive, body only just. The next morning I have no energy but my head is still thinking in the way its been conditioned to think: I can do this. I should be able to be sick and still be able to put in a top performance.

I think of the American swimmer Conor Dwyer: he was sick at NCAAs and still helped his team win the relay and swam amazingly well. If he can do it, so can I. There's hope, there's belief and then there's truth, which screams back at me from the scoreboard after the heats: nearly four seconds outside my best in 23rd. Dr. Gordon comes with me to meet the media and confirm that I've suffered a bout of acute food poisoning. "She's been up all night. She wasn't really in any state to race but she wanted to have a go," he says.

Afterwards, I go over to speak to coach Troy. He gives me one of those looks that I've seen before when he's about to deliver Troy's Truth. Where I can look forward to soothing words elsewhere, coach Troy weighs in with the kind of honesty that pays no regard to comfort: "Even if you hadn't been sick, you know you weren't honest this year and you need to figure it out and decide if you're in or not."

His delivery is cool. Some freeze when Troy's Truth hits them. I've faced it several times before over the past few years. It comes across as harsh, it can wound but the brutal bottom line is what you need to take on board to get to a better place. You can either go away, sulk and lick your wounds or stand up and admit it: coach Troy has told it like it is and given me the responsibility for and ownership of my destiny. It is in my hands to do something about it.

Behind his hard truth are years of passion and a depth of experience. Troy's warmth and compassion, his belief in each athlete who travels through his programme, are part of the success story of a man whose successes range from college honours to head coach to the US Olympic men's team, one of the most dominant forces in world sport in the past 100 years.

There are swimmers who don't realise that the likes of Americans Ryan Lochte, Elizabeth Beisel and other world champions, me included, have had our fair share of Troy's Truth. They think that success makes it easier to skirt the tough talk. Not true. Whatever level of success you achieve, owning up to and taking responsibility for falling shy of the commitment you know you need to make to get the best out of yourself is half the battle.

I'm immensely grateful to coach Troy for this. Later, when my career is done, I will experience a different side to him: he will ask me if he's been too harsh to someone. It's hard to say he has been because he knows that his approach gets the job done, gets the results. It doesn't sit well with him when he delivers a hard call but he cares enough to have people not like him for the sake of their success. Tough love, perhaps, but good love nonetheless and one that can reap rich rewards. Complete selflessness.

When I next face the media later in the day, I confirm the stomach problem but add: "It's been a bad year all round really: I've struggled to find the motivation and this will be a kick up the butt for next year." It's my way of shedding light on Troy's Truth and having it stick with me. My Shanghai world championships over, I still find the energy to party on the last night. The whole Florida crew and Britain team are out on the tiles. I dance, let go and get drunk. Very drunk. I end up on the floor in a Chinese toilet where hygiene has not been a priority. Teammate Jemma Lowe scrapes me off the floor and helps me to a taxi.

At the hotel, I feel the alcohol inside me screaming to get out! I feel so sick that I have to stop on almost every floor, get out, find a trashcan to be sick into, and call the lift again. The first stop is tricky: I stumble about a bit trying to work out where the rubbish bin is. Each floor is a blur but the standardisation of hotel layouts is a blessing: as the floors go by, I learn where to find the sick bucket, rush straight for it, vomit and wobble back to the lift. When I finally get to "my" floor I realize that I'm in the wrong place: this isn't even my hotel! Too late for all those guests about to complain about hygiene standards in this plush place. I'm in no position to worry about the trail of stomach contents I've left in my wake. Somehow I make it back to where I need to be and then find that my roommate is in bed with one of my friend's brothers.

He's one of the most adorable young boys you could meet and if I'd been sober I would have told them how pleased I was for them that they'd got together. Thankfully, I don't remember much the next morning.

The sun rises with a headache and a will to forget. Some things do stay with me: I recall that each time I needed to be sick, a knight in shining armour would leave his bed, hold my hair back until I was done, and then climb back in bed with my teammate and his partner for the night.

In some ways, all of this is life as usual on the road for a swimmer. There's one big difference for me this time. When I've let go like this at the end of the season before, it has always been because I've needed to let my hair down after many months of serious commitment. Here in Shanghai, I'm actually drowning my sorrows.

I can't tell whether this will be my last meet ever. I don't feel as though there is anything left in me to give. London 2012 is out there, a home Games but it just may be a stroke too far for me.

Doubts concealed in private thought, my parting shot to the media is more optimistic. I'd stayed awake almost all night after watching the 100m backstroke final go without me. I had a very big decision to make: quit now and move on or recommit and do it like it counts.

I tell reporters: "It's 100% commitment from hereon in. Last night there was a really big decision for me to make, whether I should do one more year or whether I should give up because this year hasn't been fun and 2009 was maybe my time. You can only do this sport to the best of your ability if you are 100% invested and this year hasn't been 100% for me."

Troy's Truth and mine, minus the lingering doubt, is now out there for all to see.

Martyn Wilby, assistant head coach at the University of Florida and personal mentor to Gemma Spofforth, on a winning partnership

Extract from an interview with Craig Lord

How did Gainesville end up choosing Gemma?

I was coached by Ian Armiger [coach at Loughborough University in England] in Darlington [England] when I was a young swimmer. I was 18 and taking my A levels at school and didn't know what I wanted to do. Ian suggested I go to the States and find myself. I said I'd go for a year - and I'm still here 30 years on. It was great to be around people like coach Troy and others who were so passionate about what they did.

Gemma came on Ian's recommendation. It was a risk to take her on. He thought she might have even retired but was looking to get back into it in the United States. If we could motivate her in the right way, he thought she could be very good. We talked with her and with Bill Sweetenham [Australian guru and Britain's performance director] and wanted to make sure he was ok with it. He said most definitely and thought she had some outstanding qualities for us to work with.

Did you see that when she arrived?

It didn't look like it at first: she was out of shape but even then you could see sparks there. Our first job was to get her in shape. Her job was to fit in and she bought in to the team concept straight up. Over here, you do it for the team. Some internationals do it for themselves but we have a different concept of how to build success for more than one or two individuals.

When did you notice her leadership qualities?

In her freshman year, when she was getting in shape, we didn't see anything outstanding. We just had a feeling that she could be very good. She then went well that season and won the NCAAs on backstroke. That was the catalyst and she grew by helping others to grow.

There were signs there all along. Fast-forward to her junior year and she was team captain and team leader and did that not only for the women but the men's team too. She has been really good at that kind of stuff. She sent out round-robins to the team, asked each person to write down something nice they saw in the next person on the list, that kind of thing. She brought people together by asking for respect and responsibility from everyone.

Your own experience kicked in when the call came through from Gemma's father to say that her mother was ailing fast. Can you explain why it was so important for you to act as speedily as you did?

I knew what it was like for me 20 odd years ago. Communication is a whole lot better these days than it was back then. There was no Skype, no Facebook, Twitter, not even mobile phones. When my mother was ill, I wondered if I should go home and my sister told me 'No, keep going, it'll be ok'. I never made it in time to say goodbye. I just wanted to make sure when Mr Spofforth called that we were not being very English and proper about it. It was important to make sure Gemma got home. So, by the miracles of airline travel these days, he called at 8.30am one morning and she was back home at 8.30am the next morning. And as it turned out, she was just in time and got to see her Mum before the end.

How has the emotional journey been for you these past few years?

It's been good because Gemma's such an honest person that you know exactly where she is at any one moment. She's very good about telling you exactly where she's at.

Probably one of best examples of that is from after her Mum's funeral. I'm dropping Gemma off at school and trying to do some small talk to see where she's at mentally, and she says: "I'm ok, this is where I am now and I'm coping but I want you to make sure that you never use my mother's passing away as motivation and I want you to let all the other coaches know that, so that they never use this as a way of motivating me." It's been like that ever since. She was going to use it herself. We never needed to mention it. That's typical Spoff.

How does she stack up as an athlete?

As a worker, she's not the best aerobic animal in the world. When you come into the pool here, you could pick out three or four people who could be world record holders. She's not one of those who would come to mind. She's got better at achieving that status because she's worked hard and consistently and she's really good at racing and knowing where her body is at. Come the faster stuff in practice, if she's not too tired, then you start to see the world-class swimmer.

Do you recall the moments after the Rome world title was won in 2009?

I was in the warm-down pool keeping my eye on the TV because I was warming someone else up. My deck pass was with Surinam. The whole suit issue had really worn on me, worn on all of us. We told everybody here "find a suit and stick with it no matter what everyone else is saying". She wanted to stick with the LZR from 2008 and I had everyone in my ear saying "I can't believe you're letting her wear the LZR and not going to put her in a full suit [2009 model]".

I started questioning it but she never did. The coaches were talking and Anthony Nesty [Olympic champion, 100m butterfly, 1988] said we'd either look like the biggest idiots or be celebrating a great day. I could not change Gemma's mind and in hindsight I'm really glad we didn't. She said 'Shut up about the suit. I'm wearing the LZR, discussion over'. In the same suit she wore to get fourth at the Beijing Olympics, she swam a second quicker for the world title. It was a phenomenal swim.

I didn't see her 'til she was getting a rub down on the massage table well after the race. She was good, she smiled, giggled. We knew what it meant, words weren't needed.

Has Gemma's experience at the Gators shaped her and has her being here shaped you?

Without a doubt. It shaped the athlete and the person. She now has the tools and experience to know if anyone finds themselves in a similar situation to those she's gone through, she'll know what to do and how to guide. She's made me a better person. She's enriched my life. I think that goes for a lot of people too.

In 2010, she maintained good form but by 2011 it had slipped away from her. What happened?

In hindsight, the warning signs were all there. We'd taken her out of what she'd done for four years and put her ... in a completely different environment . After Rome and the world title, she worked hard on the team as captain and as leader swam NCAAs and helped the Gators win it. She was then sent in a different direction in 2010.

There was gold and silver at Europeans and silver at the Commonwealth Games. She did ok maintaining and living on past form and coping with conditions in India but when she got back from Delhi, she was lost. Back here with the Gators, everyone is getting on with the rest of their life in hard training and she felt disconnected; she had no identity and felt like she was out of the group.

All the trouble and turmoil over the visa and the Green Card meant that by the time she got back after world-championship trials for Shanghai in 2011, she hadn't been part of the group for eight months or something like that. The group had changed, there were some pro athletes in the group she was in and they don't have the same team concept as that which she'd been familiar with in college.

Grief and mourning were back, too, and had all added up to the big question for her: why am I doing this? She knew that London 2012 was on the horizon but she had yet to find a way of making that mean something to her.

Were you aware as a coach that your charge was making mercy dashes as a crisis counsellor in the middle of the night sometimes?

I was aware that she was doing some work at the crisis center and that there was the odd night shift involved. I was always aware of anything like that because she would always ask 'Are you ok with that' if she was going to do something that we might have an opinion about. The other thing that gave it away as far as letting us know what it meant to her was the glow: she talked continuously about it, you knew she was really excited about it.

There was one Saturday night/Sunday morning when the phone rang at home at 3am. When your phone rings at 3am as a swim coach you know it's never someone telling you that you did a good job that day. It's something bad and my heart sank. But it was Spoff saying 'Listen, I've just saved my first life. I got called out to someone's house and I'm so fired up on adrenalin right now that it's not even funny. I just wanted to call someone and tell 'em. Good night'. That's what makes her tick. We've talked about how much of that she should do when she was training but it gave her balance and that was important.

Will you miss her when she's moved on?

Oh, yes! I think that she's going to stay here and go to graduate school and she'll be around doing coaching and teaching kids to swim but I'll miss the swimmer. The friendship will always be there.

CHAPTER 32

Back to Gainesville,
A Quinn Jones And Swim Lessons

"Success is not final, failure is not fatal: it is the courage to continue that counts"

— WINSTON CHURCHILL

Late August, back in Gainesville and I'm determined to make good my parting promise in print: to get with it, get fit and have a crack at a home Olympic Games in London next summer.

The sun's up, the day glorious and I'm off for a bike ride. It doesn't last long. I don't even see the pothole, I just know that I'm flying through the air over the handlebars. It's over in a flash. My face hits the road with a thud. I feel a searing pain and then a stinging sensation at about the same time that red becomes the only colour I can see. Dazed, I pick myself off the ground and wait for the help that a kind witness has called.

After the paramedics have patched me up, I post a couple of gruesome snapshots on Twitter and tweet: "Hey tweeps! Just chilling in the ER after falling off my bike and breaking my nose!" I update with: "Doing much better just a broken toe and broken nose!" and then "Doing much better!! Keeping me in overnight in case I have a concussion... 15 stitches, broken toe and broken nose..."

Back it Britain, it makes a headline here and there, one paper calling in a "horror bike smash". Not quite - but it does hurt a bit. After a couple of days I'm back in the water. There's been a blip in my preparation but the thing with injury or illness is that your motivation often remains intact. Mental stress, lack of drive and direction, June's death and the things I lived through on the way to Shanghai are different matters and I feel relieved to have put those behind me as best I can.

Since returning from China, I'm on the trail of all those things that fulfilled me, enriched me and helped to bring about any success in the pool, starting with commitment. There's an ulterior motive this time: If I'm not yet done as a swimmer, I'm keen to lay down the foundations for my future.

I set about experiencing life as I would like to have it pan out beyond my days in the pool, starting with the questions: who am I in this world; what is my purpose and how do I get to where I need to be? All things flow from the water. I start to eat correctly again; I put everything I have into swimming, volunteering and swim lessons with the young kids. Each experience feeds the next. I seize the day and have fun with each and every passing one that follows.

My swimming has always benefited from balance outside the pool and given that my intention is to work with underprivileged kids who struggle to find their path in life, I arrange to visit the A. Quinn Jones Center. It's a local school for children with behavioural problems along the road from the Crisis Center in Alachua not far from where I live.

I'm keen to learn more about EBDs (Emotional and Behavioural Disorders), in a place where knowledge and inspiration start with the name over the entrance. A. Quinn Jones was a prominent Gainesville educator who guided countless black students through academia in an era of segregation, disadvantage and racism.

Imagine the determination needed to do what A. Quinn Jones did at a time when being black and getting on in life through formal education were not easy bedfellows. Born in Quincy, Gadsden County, Florida, in 1893, he worked his way through school and completed high school and college in seven years at Florida A&M, earning a Bachelor of Science degree in 1915. After graduation, he accepted a teaching position at a local school; he got married, had children, earned a Master of Arts degree in 1920 from Oskaloosa College in Iowa; returned to Gainesville a year later and by 1923 was principal at Union Academy as the school moved to a new building on NW 10th Street and 7th Avenue.

Jones taught a variety of subjects, including mathematics, science, language and Latin, and was responsible for educating many of Florida's future African-American teachers. He retired in 1957 and served the community and church for the next 40 years until his death in 1997 at the grand old age of 104. Hard to fathom the monumental changes, social and otherwise, that he lived through.

I make my way to the A. Quinn Jones Center. I'm going to spend one or two hours there a week in the company of kids who don't fit in, boys and girls who spend their days going from class to detention, detention back to class on a rough road built on shaky circumstance. I believe it's never too late to set them on the right road and with each passing week I look forward to my visits as one of the highlights of my life right now.

The idea is to regale them with tales from my book of experience and have my swimming inspire the kids. They come from families who don't know how to inspire and were never taught why that is so important and how you go about achieving it. The children, some of them abuse victims, some in care homes, some in foster homes, need people to be there, to spend time with them - and listen.

I leave each session fulfilled but frustrated. If there are moments when I feel like I am useful, there are just as many when I am knocked back down to the amateur counsellor that I am. It seems that each of these children has so many things to contend with. They struggle with such an immense range of difficulties that I cannot and will not ever truly understand. One child watched his friend get shot while he was selling drugs. It's a world alien to me. The children divulge their secrets and their deepest worries to me and I find myself wanting to save them, to find a safe environment for them to grow up in.

It is hard for me to talk about my achievements, especially while I'm still a swimmer, while there are still goals and dreams and ambitions out there and there's a need to keep your feet firmly on the ground. I'm really modest and humble about it but I see the impact it has, even when I mention having swum in Beijing. The child who saw his friend shot down says: "Hey, that's cool; you've been to the Olympics?!" He wants to know more, he's all ears, his head no longer down, his gaze no longer averted. He's engaged, interested. Perhaps he will be inspired and motivated too.

It's not always an easy experience. There are some pretty tough kids here but I never feel threatened because the dean is with me and he's earned everyone's respect. He always "has my back", as the Americans say when someone watches out for you. I get the feeling that he'd like me to go further. I'm conscious that there's more I might say once I've moved on from my racing days and I too can let go a little more. There's more advantage to be had from talking to the kids about specific achievement but right now, I'm an active swimmer and have a certain way of being that helps me to make it all work, feet on the ground, expectation in check, targets ahead, cloud-busting left for history if and when it happens.

If swimming helps me to help the kids here, then what I'm learning at A. Quinn Jones is how to whet my appetite for swimming once more: after each visit I return to the pool happy, fulfilled and ready to give of my best. I'm getting back the love and my work with a whole different group of kids to the A. Quinn Jones crew is part and parcel of it. Wilby's wife, Jill, runs the swim school lessons and has asked me if I'd like to help out.

You bet! It's one of the best decisions I ever made. The two hours I spend in the learning pools down the far end of the outdoor training facility, blue skies above, the sparkle and splash of sunlit water a chorus to the bubbling tune of children's laughter, are among my favourite moments in life. Their hilarious questions and the sheer joy on the bright young faces are balsam for the soul,

I take kids aged three to six. They start with "pencils and pancakes", the pencil reflected in the straight arms they stretch above their heads, the pancake the act of putting your hands stacked one on top of the other like pancakes (not palm to palm as in clapping). Somewhere down the line of learning, a switch is flicked and an arm will come out of the water and swing across the surface. It's their first stroke as a swimmer. A light goes on. To be there at the dawn of skill and tell a child how well they've done fills me with energy.

I nestle my face against the little girl's cheek, cup her head in my hand. She trusts me and floats on her back. Gradually, I let go and she's on her own. I catch her when she realises she's free. "Amazing - do you know what you just did?! You floated on your back all by yourself!" Beaming smile. "Again!" Swimming is not just about racing but about loving it and showing the kids that they can love it too, the very first steps to full strokes in swimming create meaning and accomplishment in the lives of these children.

There are three kids in the lesson today. Two love it, one says he hates it. I ask him why. "Because I have to get changed," comes the reply. I laugh out loud. I smile up at the smiling parents sitting in a row of folk taking pride in the progress unfolding before their eyes.

I'm reading a book right now that asks: "What's your driving force; what do your friends think your driving force is?" Subconsciously, I've been asking that of myself for a while now and answering it by filling my life with things that make me happy.

One of them is Decker, the gorgeous pitbull I named after Wilby's favourite British chocolate bar. I picked him out at a rescue home. He was very thin, unhealthy and on a list to be put down. Wilby had said "no pets" before the Olympics but I convince him all is well: Decker is going to be looked after (on loan) to my housemates until the swimming job is done. I'm not sure Wilby believes me.

I've fooled myself and others in a number of ways in recent times when it's come to commitment. I'm much more solid on the future. The answer is very clear to me: the more I see the children I'm working with grow, the more it inspires me to grow and the happier I am. It's not a question of doing something for the money. Yes, we all need to eat and we need a place to live but the reward is to be found in doing something you love, something that drives you.

I'm standing on the deck in the evening sun. A child looks up from the sparkling water and smiles broadly. He's just taken the next step and had fun doing it. I've helped make this day a better one for him and for the kids in the water with him. Just what I gain from that is hard to put into words. I feel warm inside. It's not only emotional, it's physical.

The secret to fulfilled lives, to happiness, isn't out there somewhere, it's right here inside us, waiting for us to unlock it. We are the key. We are our own key. I'm learning something big about myself: by helping others to get the best out of themselves, I'm lighting their way and in turn inviting light into my own life. It's what A. Quinn Jones did. I hope that I can walk a parallel path.

the first thing I see. I feel rage not sadness. I'm taking it personally. Why? Why does this stuff happen all the time? There is no reason for someone so young to suffer all of this and die. No reason for her child to be left like this. What purpose does it serve?

At the pool, I punch the water with each stroke, taking my anger out on an element that has been my friend but today will serve as a punchbag for my pain and anger. I don't even feel that I can tell people about Vicky because she's not close family as such. I can't broach it with people who may well think "What... so how many more times do we have to comfort her for the same thing?" I know, of course, that that's not how any of my family, friends, coaches and teammates would react but I feel unable to even get as far as burdening them with it this time.

Mum and June have become a practised routine that ends with a stiff upper lip. Vicky is different. Fury burns in me.

* * *

Just as a black cloud can blot out the sun on a hot August day, doubt shrouds this former champion's positive spirit. I'm in turmoil.

Positive spirit, strength of character and a full heart are the cherries on top of an athlete's cake after months of hard-baked work and dedication On race day, the inner voice sets the tone.In this final stage before the 2012 Olympic trials, my inner voice tells me "you can't do this". Expectations weigh heavily. I feel numb. I feel nothing, no passion, no drive, for weeks. I'm on auto-pilot, merely existing in the pool, not striving in it. My preparation is very far from perfect but as coaches Troy and Wilby remind me, I have shown up, I have been consistent in that, I have latent, retained fitness, conditioning, experience and the ability to find the right tools at the right moment. Time to go, paint a smile on and face my fate.

As I prepare to leave Florida for London, the words of my housemate and fellow crisis counsellor David Marra from a year ago come to mind: "You are a swimmer, but that isn't who you are . you are an amazing counsellor, a wonderful daughter, a great sister, an amazing friend, and then an athlete. Whether you get first place or last in any race you've already succeeded in a major part of your life because you've overcome adversity and you've touched the lives of so many people."

I use it as a comfort blanket to wrap myself in just in case I miss the boat. Then, something happens on the way to the London 2012 pool. From the moment I land in Britain, I'm acutely aware that the nation has woken up to the Games. There are posters and signs and symbols, Olympic pages in the papers, talk of the big show coming to a screen near you. The Games are everywhere as I make my way into town.

My arrival at St Pancras Station is a pivotal moment. London always has a buzz, a smell, a sound about it but there is more to it than that this time. I look up. Floating high above me are the five Olympic rings. One chance, one chance in a lifetime. Guess I'll take it. The dream reawakens. I really do want this journey after all.

It's Sunday morning on a crisp and cold March day out at Stratford at the heart of a transformed East London. Just a few years ago, it was a derelict, crumbling wasteland here. Now, there are hotels, one of Europe's biggest shopping centres and chic flats that will house teams during the Games before being handed over as housing for the people who will live the London 2012 legacy.

The Olympic pool fills the horizon, its roof like the upturned belly of a blue whale, its fins the stands where 17,000 or so people will roar on those lucky enough to make it back here in July. I am still finding it hard to place myself in that picture as I race in the heats of the 100m backstroke. Later in the day I'm back for the semi-finals and even now at this late hour, I feel numb and ask myself: do I care?

The ability to fathom the mind is one thing. The ability to control it is another. To be the master of your own mind is to possess a very powerful tool. The voice inside my head might say "I don't want her to beat me", or in other words "I want to win". The better approach is "I want to beat her": there is no negative. The first approach is a world I cannot control, I cannot do anything about how my opponent races; the second approach is a world I control, my performance unfolding within my scope and expectation.

This simple act of understanding my positive inner voice is the key to booking my place on the Olympic team. I don't claim to be able to control the mind or even understand it. However, through the power of imagery and positive inner voice I flip a doubt-filled preparation 180 degrees. Night to day.

I make the final and the very act of doing so turns up the dial of desire. I'm now free and able to admit to myself that I want it. I refuse to finish second.

After speaking to that theme in the mixed zone, I tell reporters that I find the ceiling lights, set in large round recesses above us, a little distracting. It's something I'll have to get used to. Nothing too juicy in that, you might have thought but the salivating media that follows is Olympic in proportion.

A breeze becomes a maelstrom. A throw-away comment becomes "an Olympic crisis", the London 2012 pool panned as "awful" by a world champion "blinded by the light". Total exaggeration.

The only thing I can do is shrug it off and refocus. I do just that, remembering what Troy and Wilby told me about the tools I have to get me through when others might falter. In the call room before the race, there are a lot of pale, serious, even scared faces. For me, given all that's happened, this is the easy bit, the fun bit, the chance to show what you've got. I'm nervous but not overly so. This is my sanctuary. I know I can cope better here than anyone else around me. I've proved that time and again.

I'm unaware of anyone else in the race. I look up and take in my victory and time: 1min 00.19sec. Others have talked about being on cloud nine when they've made the Olympic team. I just feel relieved. Not even my Dad has known how to be around me because of the vibes of uncertainty flowing from me. He's known that I've been thinking of quitting and while he hasn't said anything, I know that he didn't want me to miss out on what could be the biggest moment of my career.

I'm far away from where I have been and could be but it's good enough: I'm going to a home Games. Lizzie Simmonds, my long-time partner in the international call room, isn't so lucky. In the blanket finish, Georgia Davies is 0.02sec away from me and inside the Olympic cut, Lizzie 0.22sec slower. Her stronger event, the 200m, is yet to come. Doubt, now banished for me, stands in her way.

I, too, have the 200m to come but that is now secondary. I've left everything in the pool in the 100m, fighting through agony in the last 10m; I refused to yield, staved off retirement, given myself something much bigger to fight for.

With a keen sense of accomplishment, I leave London for Gainesville with my drive, motivation and mind back to best. I'm more aware than ever that I've been woefully lacking in those areas since the beginning of the year. I feel as though I have nothing to lose and everything to gain.

There's no stopping me. I get straight back into training, take Decker for long walks, swim a lot, run a lot, get really fit and feel proud of myself. Then, travelling to a camp, I injure my shoulder and have to spend the whole time working on kick only. It may turn out to be a blessing in disguise: my legs are getting really strong.

A few weeks later, Craig Lord comes out to visit. I tell him I'm back on track. He wants proof. I show him my computer screensaver: the scoreboard from the Beijing Olympics is back, the worst place of all, 4th, there to remind me that I want more. I'd put it back in place after qualifying at trials.

On my phone are a whole list of reminders and prompts:

- *put 100% in, which was harder than I thought it would be*
- *get back into Rome shape*
- *do not eat chocolate*
- *have a professional attitude*
- *go blonde. then go back brown again (I like change)*
- *do a lot more recovery foam rolls (trigger points, builds muscle) and flexibility exercises*
- *supplement regime.*

Nutrition was my last card to play: I'd never really been into supplements but I was determined to leave no stone unturned for this final push and I'm already in far better shape than I was at trials. My house is full of triggers: from the food in the fridge to the absence of things that won't help and on to the bright orange, spiky foam roll that I've left on a speaker next to the TV in the living room as a constant reminder to use it.

I'm having a massage once a week and looking after myself in every conceivable way to make sure the hard work in the water is balanced with recovery. I'm feeling stronger that I have done since 2009-10. That's down to my work with weights coach Matt Delancey, all 300lbs of him. He has me lifting, doing throws, "hang cleans", jumps, a lot of jumps, and everything else designed to build strength.

Matt really pushes me and motivates me by telling me he hasn't seen me in this kind of shape since 2009. Wilby says something similar: I'm working a lot with snorkels that have a restriction in them to make lungs work harder; I'm running stadiums,100 steps at a time and eight times over. I'm boxing and going rock climbing too.

It all contributes to a great sense of turnaround, of happiness. I've talked about the cyclical nature of being happy before in my chats with sports psychologist and friend Spencer Wood. He'd explained to me that there is often a problem when expectation is too high, because that makes you feel less confident. The level of confidence is not the issue. I've now brought expectation down from "Olympic gold medal" to the same level as the confidence in me. I feel a lot happier, more balanced, more able to talk to people one on one. That is not to say my personal expectations have lowered but I have placed them in the context of my preparation and process.

The other trigger to feeling good is living in the present. I don't need to be thinking about what's happened, what's gone on in the past two years, don't need to think about not having touched the wall first in the last two years or whether I'll touch the wall first at the Olympics. I simply need to think about doing the best I can each and every day and enjoying the moment.

It's not always easy to do that. How do you stop yourself dreaming about the future? Yet to do so may cause you to set your heart on a specific outcome and if things don't pan out you'll be disappointed. That in turn may well lead you to let another chance pass you by at a time when you're feeling low.

Perhaps the best time to lay down plans is when you're feeling good, when you're happy. I'm never so happy as when I'm working to help others, not just myself. On that score, today, this very moment as I write, is a great one: I just got word that I've been accepted for a postgraduate course in psychology and counselling at the University of Florida. I've already been talking to someone about working for a non-profit organisation focused on kids who have been underprivileged and on the wrong tracks.

A good thought. I'm taking one day at a time.

CHAPTER 34

Grant and Emotional Healing

"In this world, there is nothing scarier than trusting someone. But there is also nothing more rewarding"

— BRAD MELTZER

In this happy time on the way to London 2012, I exorcise one of the demons of the past few years: men. Or rather, how I deal with them. I take time to spend a romantic night on the beach with a good man. The evening starts out with me wanting to take it further than the friendship and bond we've had since I was a freshman at college five years ago. Nothing happens. It's obvious that he doesn't feel the same spark as I do. That turns out to be the best thing that could have happened.

Grant Johnson and I have been close since we started at the University of Florida. He lost his Dad and he understood how I was feeling about Mum. We talked a lot about it. At each new twist and bend on the emotional roller coaster I've been riding, he's been there for me. We've had an amazing friendship, sometimes intense but never intimate: he always had a girlfriend.

A 200m freestyle swimmer, his first SEC Championships also marked my debut. We were both sick. Isolated from the team to keep as many healthy as possible, we travelled to the meet together and became friends. We enjoyed each other's company, had much in common, talked a lot and wrote novel-length emails to each other for five years.

There were times when I felt totally drained and exhausted after an email exchange because I had purged myself of everything that was happening, exorcised my demons, got something out of my system. In one mail I tell Grant: "It's strange because these emails are like an addiction, I need my fix even though I know I might feel drained after; I cannot sit on your email and let it fester because my mind starts racing with things I can reply with ... Our emails are like buried treasure, hidden gems deep underground with sentimental value, buried so only you and I can find them."

He feels the same way. We are both better at writing down how we feel than standing up and saying it. The closeness of our exchanges leads me to the brink of making another mistake. I formed bad habits through my immature approach to men at a time of chaos and confusion. Heart, mind, love, lust and all things in between were thrown into the glass left empty by Mum's passing. A dangerous cocktail.

Reading back the emails I exchanged with Grant, it is easy to see how I thought we might be linked romantically. I believed that he felt the same way. Back in autumn 2011, after being washed up in the wreckage of the Shanghai world championships, Grant was a pillar of strength, a shoulder to cry on. Our friendship was so solid. I'd been able to tell him anything. He was the one I had been able to turn too. Whatever the subject, whatever the taboo. He was the closest I'd ever come to having a confidante; we shared a level of emotion built on common grief. I trusted him with things I had never told anyone else and he in turn trusted me with deeply private thoughts.

In one mail Grant recalls a scene that haunts: the doctor shakes his head, lowers his gaze to the floor; his Dad's life has ended. The scene plays out in his head at the pace of a slow-motion movie clip. Grant writes about hugging his Dad and feeling the warmth leave the body of the man who helped bring him into this world. He has to end the mail at that point because he was sitting in Starbucks and didn't want to start blubbing in his latte, he tells me.

He asks for a shoulder to cry on when he's next up from Tampa on a visit to Gainesville. I'm moved deeply. I identify with what he is going through.

There had never been any hint of physical relationship yet there's a fine line between friendship and love. In the past year I've felt a sense of creeping frustration. I wonder about the nature and depth of his feelings for me. Come May 2012, the Olympics looming ever larger, there's an undertone to the relationship that I hadn't noticed before. Perhaps it was never there. I like him but I feel I'm not getting enough from him, our platonic friendship no longer satisfying a deeper need in me. I tell him so.

He writes back:

Gemma your words mean so much to me, and they give me so much strength. I get goosebumps whenever i think about coming up to see you and having one of our bear hugs!! I draw a great deal of my strength from you and thinking about your life and what you've been through and the person you've become. It's funny that you say my strength is inspirational, because I feel the same way about your strength!

Gemma, you will always have me in your life. Always and forever. I love you, as well, so much it bursts from my eyeballs when I see you, and I intend to have you in my life and inside my heart for long after you and I have left this plane of existence. We definitely have something unique and beautiful between us. I feel like we can relate to each other on things that I just can't with other people. As well your brutal honesty wrapped in a fluffy shell of tough-love is usually the best medicine I can get, lol. You are right, in that I am going through a bit of a time right now and unfortunately I'm not at a point in my life when I can give enough of myself to anyone. I've decided to forgo a romantic relationship with anyone until I feel more stable and balanced with myself emotionally, mentally and spiritually. You help me so much with everything you do, it's perfect exactly the way it is now. You know I love you and I will not treat our friendship any differently than I always have. I still need you in my life too, and I intend to keep you in it forever. I reply:

I meant everything I said and it's taken me 3 years of crazy "dating" or whatever you call it, a second death, and a year of finding myself to know that I am now ready for something real, ready for someone who loves me and ready to love and respect myself before giving myself completely to said person. I really hope you have a better journey than I did. I know the love in your heart is pure gold and when you feel stable enough to give it to someone they will be the luckiest person on the planet. With a well developed brick wall around my heart protecting it from pain, I can safely say that, although feeling vulnerable since my last email, I am 100% on the same page and our friendship will never change. I was terrified that admitting my feelings would change us but I know that the bond that we have has grown from a root and it will take an awful lot of lumberjacks to tear this tree down.

In the words of a very wise woman "Keep smiling and the world will smile with you, aim high darling and you will reach your dreams." She is with me every day, in my heart, in my words and in my smile. She protects me from pain and laughs with me. I have had countless days and nights of relentless sobbing, I have had more nights and days of remembering her strength, using her strength to help others and mirroring her to keep her spirit alive. Each day brings a different emotion and each day I bury it deep within me so that others can continue smiling and laughing with me. (what I am trying to say is, the strength you see and love is a strength she gave me, but deep within me there is pain and sorrow, there is fear and regrets, there is a huge hole in my heart that can never be filled, there is a search for a life she would be proud of - and there is a constant wall around my heart to prevent people seeing those emotions because I cannot allow myself to see them either.) One day I will find the strength to remove the wall but until that day all I can do is keep smiling and have the world smile with me.

Despite that exchange I still feel as though he's flirting with me, leading me on. I feel stress rise in me every time I get another text message from him. It was never meant to be like this. He visits Gainesville for the weekend, sends signals, massages my head while sat behind me in the car, tells me he loves me and tells me how beautiful I look.

After he's left, I send him a clear message: stop leading me on. The long text reads:

So you may or may not have noticed that I am not being myself around you .... And I know it's not fair to you but I am passive aggressive to say the least and it will manifest itself in the smallest things. You were told on multiple occasions that I had feelings for you more than friends and you continued to say things and do things that would be perceived as "leading me on" and I have now got to the point where I'm completely over those feelings and you are still saying and doing those things and now they frustrate me. You were given a part of me, I shared some of my most vulnerable parts with you. Now a wall has gone back up. Those parts of me are not available for you until I can learn to trust your authenticity. I don't really want to talk about it... This is where I'm at right now and I would appreciate it if you could respect that.

He replies:

I did notice, I am sorry I hurt you.

We don't speak again until late June. By then I'm on the cusp of leaving for London but after the Games, our friendship returns to being amazing. That is made possible by the understanding I've reached with myself. I figure out that I wasn't into him in that way at all (or if I was, there's no spark there now). It is just a friendship. I needed to take a step backwards, think, breathe and then know that I share a strong emotional connection with a man with whom I have no need to have a physical relationship with. Our soulmates could be our girlfriends. It's ok for a man to be a soulmate and a "boy-girlfriend".

Grant, who has a busy life as a voice coach for actors and a leader in the boy-scout movement, finds time to visit me after the Olympics in England. Our friendship is now solid, any physical connection gone. A deep emotional understanding remains. It feels wonderful. I have learnt from the Hobbit, from Philip, from Jay, from a series of what I called obsessions at the time (though that is not quite the right word). And I have learnt much more from Grant, my lifelong friend. Perhaps if I had said to Hobbit what I have been able to say to Grant, had the conversation about leading me on, Hobbit might have said the same as Grant - but I never gave him that chance.

Paul William Young explains it perfectly in his novel, *The Shack*, in a conversation between God and his protagonist, Mack: "[Mack], if you and I are friends, there is an expectancy that exists within our relationship. When we see each other or are apart, there is an expectancy of being together, of laughing and talking. That expectancy has no concrete definition; it's alive and dynamic and everything that emerges from our being together is a unique gift shared by no one else. But what happens when we change that expectancy to an expectation? Suddenly, law has entered into our relationship and you are now expected to perform in a way that meets my expectations. Our living friendship rapidly deteriorates into a dead thing with rules and requirements."

That summarises my life with men in one paragraph. It emphasises the unreasonable expectation I place on these unsuspecting folk as I try to control the outcome and force a relationship. That has created a false impression. I've been impatient to force what cannot be forced. If the spark is keen, the flame will follow. I've been blowing the spark out. I have anchored myself to a way of being. Free of such ties, I will not drift away. I will still be here but in a safer, happier place.

CHAPTER 35

End Games

"Where you invest your love you invest your life"

— Mumford and Sons

I've been so focused. A Quinn Jones, swim lessons with the kids, home life but beyond all of that these past three months, the things that stand out are the hard work, the dedication, the recommitment to a dream, the land training, the work in the water, the striving to get back to peak fitness, the belief that I have good swimming in me yet and I can make a home Olympic Games count.

On this aquatic journey, I've ended up in many a dead-end, been forced to make U-turns, been frustrated, sad, weak, strong, confident, vulnerable, at the lowest of lows and the highest of highs. My dream has never faltered, even if the motivation to do the things required to live the dream has at times been tossed on the rocks in a storm of confounding circumstance.

It is at such times that you have to adapt, find a new path and ways to rekindle the flame, keep the dream alive. I have become addicted to rock-climbing in the ascent to my second Olympics. It has pushed my mind and body to its limits. I've experienced moments of soaring elation in reaching the top of a climb. My grip, my strength and starts in the pool have benefited from the challenges I've taken on outside the pool.

In the water, I have a new training partner, Kaitlin Frehling. We go head to head in 200m freestyle tests. We fuel each other's passion. One day she mentions my "laser-eyes". She explains how she feels that my eyes burn through her when we make eye contact when racing. She sees how much I want it. She feels both intimidated and inspired as we make each other better day-in, day-out.

It's good to gain new skills and then feed your passion and dream with them. "Reach for the moon and even if you miss you'll land among the stars," is what my Mum liked to say.

The moon remains an Olympic gold medal. The fact that I will be racing at London 2012 has already brought me back to the Olympic orbit. I try not to talk too much about it with my housemates in Gainesville. They so much want me to do well. They use positive phrases such as "... when you bring home the gold medal ...". I can't approach it like that. Yes, I want to win but the process of doing everything I need to do to place myself in the realm of that possibility is what I have to focus on.

I start packing for London later than I normally would for a big competition. I don't have much to take because I'll be handed a whole load of kit - suits, track suits, shoes, t-shirts, goggles, hats, towels, pool shoes, bag and more - when I get to Britain. I'm not as enthusiastic as I usually am. My bag sits on the bed, Decker plonked on top of it. I don't want to leave him. I'd rather stay home. That may sound bizarre when you think of the chance-in-a-lifetime event I'll be representing my country at a couple of weeks from now. Even so, I don't feel excited.

I look around at the house I've bought here in Gainesville and listen to the silence from the other rooms. I won't be gone for that long but I know I'll miss David Marra and my former Gator teammate and one of my closest friends, Anna-Liisa Pold, who swam for Estonia in 2008. I'll miss chatting with Nelle Glasser. I'll miss our family dinners, the ones where I play "mom", as the Americans say, and David plays dad to our two girls in the organized chaos of four independent lives brought together under one roof.

It's not the set of Friends; it's much more than that. It is a dedication to one another's life, a burning family bond.

Melancholy leaves me once I get to the airport. It's really happening now. I start to record my journey - and will do so in words, pictures and videos throughout the Games, documenting and saving every little detail along the way. My diary starts with a first-class flight home to England. It's been on my bucket list for ages and there's no better time to do it than on the way to the Olympic Games in London. I've got my cuddly pig, the one Anna gave me, my water bottle, my headphones. I'm finally excited to be on the way. I'm open to experience.

The bond I have formed with Anna, sewn like the seams of this pig I'm clutching, warms my spirit. Friendship so deep allows people space to be exactly who they want to be.

On arrival in Britain, I hook up with the team. There's a stop at the Olympic pool and Athletes' Village to soak it up, get our kit and make the Olympic pool our own in heart and mind. Next stop, Edinburgh. We fly over the beautiful, green and rolling hills of Scotland for a holding camp before we return to London for the start of battle.

Right up until the 100m backstroke, I am 100 per cent sure that this will be my last race. I am done with this career. This will be my last stand. I should have stuck to that but hesitation, a change of heart, creeps in somewhere on the way to the final.

In the water, something stands in my way. I'm even thinking 'well, maybe I'll go to 2014 and do the Commonwealth Games'. I should not let this happen. The Olympic final is no place for doubt or secondary thought or feelings about the future. It is a one-stop, one-chance mission of singular focus. I will always wonder whether the 0.37sec by which I missed the podium would have been wiped away had I stuck to my guns and told myself "This is it - leave everything you've got in this lane right here, right now because this journey ends here this very day".

My time is my best since my world title in Rome back in 2009. I'm one of only a handful of Britain swimmers to go better at the Games than I went in this same pool at trials. But 59.20 leaves me shy of where I want to be. The champion is 17-year-old wonder girl Missy Franklin, from Colorado. She's having a great meet and will leave London with five medals, two of them gold. The 100m crown is hers in 58.33 seconds, Australia's Emily Seebohm on 58.68, the bronze going to Japan's Aya Terakawa in 58.83. I leap across the lane rope to hug Missy, a phenomenal athlete but above all a great person.

And that's the point. The things I will take away with me from this amazing place and all the others I've been to along the way are the people. The sound of a home crowd, a roar that sends the hair on the back of my neck standing to attention, will reverberate in me long after the Olympic lights go out at the London Aquatics Centre.

I look up at a sea of red, white and blue, a roll of humanity in stands that seem to soar into the sky. I wave in appreciation of their support and take a moment to think of those who have helped me on this journey. I've always said it's the journey and not the destination that counts. I am disappointed with the result but everything happens for a reason. I have had a ball, swimming has been my life, my passion, my dream, my destiny for so long. I have been to the stars and back and down into the deepest of wells but I leave this pool with my love of this sport intact. Reborn in fact.

Fifth is what I got, four years after fourth. Not right here and right now but later it will occur to me that if I had got a medal my world might not be the same. I might not be in graduate school, might not ride the wave that I catch after the Games are done, learn new things to love, lead the life I lead and have the chance to be a "normal" person.

I'm grateful for what I have had and what I have, for the love of swimming that brought so much to my life, that shaped and moulded me in ways I had never dreamt of. It has placed me in the path of some of the finest examples of what makes our world so special: people.

Gregg Troy, head coach, University of Florida and London 2012 USA men's team, on Gemma Spofforth

Extract from interviews with Craig Lord

Can you recall what she was like when she arrived in Gainesville?

When Gemma came here, she was sick, she was on the verge of being out of the sport. But she had some good tools and a great background built when she was younger. Even so, from our perspective there was a lot of doubt because you could look her way and say hers was a career going down the tubes. Ian Armiger [coach at Loughborough University in England] was good at recommending her and said she had the right mind to be good. Bill Sweetenham [Australian guru and performance director of Britain at the time] identified her as someone he thought had the tools to be very good.

For us, she was a calculated risk, a very good one as it turned out. The intangible that we didn't know at the time was that Gemma is just a wonderful person. She's a great team person, she has a good feel for and understanding of other people. All the hardships relative to her mother's illness and passing contributed to making her a better athlete.

What are her strengths as an athlete?

Gemma is a talented young lady but she has developed the types of talents that do not come naturally - and that is her strength. She works really hard and often swims really slow in [training] season and sometimes in practice to be able to cope and to master technique and make necessary adjustments for her to be as successful as she has been. I'm not sure that if she swam as fast as she could have done all the time through every competition she would have been as successful.

An example in practice is that she's mostly last when we do a 15x200 metre set but for her that set is a great day's work. She accrues slowly but surely. She's had a lot of pressure to deal with, so to be good at every single competition and cope with everything else would probably have done her more hurt than good. She's a big girl. To get the athletic body she has and to get to where she's gotten took an awful lot of work and it also means that it takes her a long time to rest and recover so she can race fast. She needs hard work and she needs really good rest.

Gemma could be a little more refined in the way she goes about certain things. She can be rough - technically speaking - sometimes but while she could be better in that area you could make the case that she if we'd have done less work and got her to be better technically, we wouldn't have achieved the same level of result.

Beyond her work ethic, what are the qualities that contribute to her being a winner?

Her college accomplishments have probably been the most important thing for Gemma the person, not just the swimmer. Beyond what she's accomplished as an athlete, she is a genuinely good person. The caring side of her helped make the people around her better too because of it. Consequently, the whole team was supportive of her when she was going through all those hard times.

She and Ryan [Lochte, Olympic 400m medley and 4x200m freestyle champion at London 2012] both train in very good competitive groups: the biggest tribute I could pay either of them is that in those groups there is very, very little envy and no disgruntlement towards them because of their success, because their work ethic is so high and because their approach to other people has been so good.

When Gemma helped captain the Gators to the SEC title in 2009 and was then captain when the girls won NCAAs in 2010, she asked each swimmer to write something down good about the next person on the team list and it's hard to recall a season when it was so quiet when it came down to any trouble on the team. She handled it before it got to us and helped her peers to maturity. She came up with a lot of that stuff herself. She has great leadership qualities. She has a fine ability to embrace people.

Even when it comes at her own expense?

Quite frankly, four years before we would not have imagined she would have got herself into the place she was in in 2010. She had the unique opportunity at NCAAs to become the first in history to win the same event for a fourth time. She missed out when she was second in the 200m backstroke after having won it three times. I really think that her commitment to the team and to others that year cost her the prize.

I will also say this: that same meet, she swam the medley and all four relays and did a great job in them and the 200 back was on the last day of the competition. A combination of her enthusiasm to the team, her commitment to others and swimming all those events probably hurt a little bit but I'm not so certain that those things were the same things that made her so successful in Rome [2009 world title in the 100m]. She was in great shape that summer. I said to Wilby that I thought she had a 57.5sec in her but I sent her with him and she went a 58.12 world record. It got the job done. She did that in the Speedo LZR suit of 2008. Had she put on the full rubber suit before they were banned from 2010, she would have gone 57.5.

She didn't want to wear the 2010 suit. How did you feel about that?

I just didn't feel comfortable with any of it. Our philosophy all through that era was that Speedo was our sponsor but that the athlete had the option to do what they wanted. My personal view is that you go to the meet knowing what you're going to wear, what you feel comfortable with, knowing that you're ready to go. You don't make a change. That's what Gemma stuck to.

How do you describe your relationship with swimmers?

I probably get more from them than they get from me. Basically, they're good people, they work hard, they're fun to be around and they have high expectations. The way I see it, it's my job to help them get the best out of themselves, not just in the pool but in terms of the qualities that make them rounded, successful individuals in whatever walk of life they choose after the swimming stops.

Epilogue

"Laughter is sunshine, it chases winter from the human heart"

– MITCH ALBOM

September 21, 2012. It's official. I send my statement to Craig Lord at The Times: time to move on. No more early morning alarm, no more gruelling training sessions. I'm done. I've taken up a voluntary coaching position at the University of Florida, will focus on my grad school studies and work towards a future in counselling and helping young people find a good path in life.

My official parting words are these: "I have had a very turbulent career and I feel that I cannot top a home crowd in London or a world record in Rome. I cannot top the experiences I have had and most importantly the friends I have made through the sport. When it comes down to it, the races and competition are not what will stay with me, the people and friends I have met and made will stay with me forever.

"I would love to thank everyone who has made this journey possible, specifically the unconditional support and love my Dad has given me over these years. The patience my brother has shown with his world-travelling sister. And the fantastic coaching I have received from each and every one of my coaches.

"I've started a new life. I'd like to work with under-privileged kids who need that structure in their lives, who need sport or something like that in their lives. To be able to create that avenue for the kids, one that I was so lucky to have myself because I had a fortunate childhood, is something that really motivates me."

Among the tributes reported is this from coach Troy: "She's a great leader, a motivator. She was phenomenal at bringing people together, at bonding, so much so that I even had her work with the men as a surrogate captain. Her work ethic is so high and her approach to other people has been so good."

Ryan Lochte, my fellow Gator and Olympic 400m medley champion for the US, is quoted as saying: "The things that she's had to overcome in her life really made me look up to her. It's just amazing when you lose a loved one like that and still be driven and determined to go out there and do your best. She's been a friend and an inspiration for a lot of people."

I hope I always will be, just as others have been there for me in that way. There are new mountains to climb. I plan ascents of the seven great peaks, starting with Rainier through to Everest, as soon after 2015 as funding will allow.

As I read through these chapters in readiness for publication, I'm aware of just how much I've grown these past six years. If my story, my experience, which is not as painful as the lives of others I've come across on my journey, can help others better cope and understand what they are going through, then it will have served a good purpose. In counselling, we learn not to give people false hope. I would never wish to do that but I think this voyage of mine has proved that you can be at the bottom of the well and find hope, real hope.

I'm still learning, still growing, self-doubt still comes creeping but I know I can learn from it and I know that along the way I can pass on wisdom that may be helpful to others.

I spoke to Dad a few weeks ago and told him about my self-doubt. He replied: "You're just like your mother. She was full of self-doubt too."

I am closest to her when I look out of the window at the warm light of the sun or sit out in it and close my eyes. It is a comfort to me that I am starting to be like her. She was my morning wakeup call, my comfort blanket, my truth, my pillar, my fan, my listening ear, my shoulder to lean on, my glass of water, my reflected smile. I will always miss her being there for a hug, a kind and wise word, a laugh. But she is not gone. I haven't really lost her because she is in me, with me and in everything I do. I still feel she is here.

I love you Mum.

Where to get help

All that said, should you ever find yourself in a time of crisis, know that you are not alone:

Call:

United States of America: 1-800-SUICIDE (1-800-784-2433) or 1-800- TALK (1-800-273-8255)
www.suicidehotlines.com

International:
www.suicidehotlines.com/international.html

United Kingdom: 08457 90 90 90* (UK); 1850 60 90 90* (ROI)
www.samaritans.org

Australia: tel. 13 11 14
www.lifeline.org.au

Printed in Great Britain
by Amazon.co.uk, Ltd.,
Marston Gate.